TACKLE READING

TACKLE READING

by

Kathryn Starke

Foreword by Ryan J. Brant,
President, Positive-Strides.Org

ISBN: 978-0-9769737-5-1
Library of Congress Control Number: 2016912326

Printed in the United States

 Published by Creative Minds Publications
www.creativemindspublications.com

Table of Contents

Foreword By Ryan J. Brant

(President/CEO of Positive-Strides.Org)

Playing sports and education often go hand in hand. However, for many athletes, myself included, going to school seemed like a necessary evil on the way to grander aspirations of becoming a professional, highly paid sports celebrity. The reality, in most cases, is that even good athletes often don't make the cut to a career of fame and fortune and even if they do make it - many do not have a back-up plan when playing sports is no longer an option. Whether it is from a play-ending injury or retirement after a successful career, many athletes, having sacrificed or ignored their education, are hard pressed to find good jobs, make a living, or contribute to society when playing sports ends for whatever reason.

We've heard it before but READING is fundamental and education, no matter what your goal in life, is the key to success. Even if you are the best on the playing field and struggle in the classroom, reading is the key to becoming a well-educated, well-rounded, successful adult. It opens the door to your imagination and helps you discover new things. Reading, whether you are a great reader or not, helps you develop and grow. Too many young athletes don't understand the importance of reading and how it can help you develop and increase your vocabulary, your communication skills and the plain ability to carry on an interesting conversation with another person.

As a former Division 1 lacrosse player, I was heavily recruited by many prestigious colleges around the country to play lacrosse. It was a heady experience and I felt, not only on top of the world, but pretty invincible. If given the choice between playing and reading, I would choose being on the playing field hands down to sitting down to read a book—any book! But, suddenly, after 4 knee injuries/surgeries and a back surgery due to overcompensating for my bad knee, I found myself in a very strange situation, one that I had not prepared myself for because, let's face it, as a young athlete I was (or thought I was) invincible! Unable to play and not sure what to do with my newly found "free" time, I became depressed and started to let my school work slide. Fortunately, I had a great support system in my family and friends and I eventually saw the light at the end of the tunnel and realized that there was, indeed, more to life than just playing sports. I was able to turn a tough situation into a positive one by creating a non-profit, called Positive-Strides.org to help young injured athletes like myself cope with play-ending injuries. Our mission at Positive-Strides.org is to ADVOCATE-EDUCATE and SUPPORT injured youth athletes in a variety of ways – from Injury Prevention and Nutritional Seminars to Mentorship Programs. Positive-Strides.org stresses the importance of education and, of course, reading.

Reading is one of the most important tools in life to be successful and I find that the more I read, the more I learn and the more I am able to make a positive contribution to those who I serve as well as friends and family. This book is filled with stories that will entertain, encourage, and, even amuse you. Written by some awesome athletes who have made the connection between reading and success, I think you will be inspired to read more. As an athlete or just a "regular" person, we like to be challenged or strive to reach the goal line. I challenge you to read this book, discuss some of the stories with family and friends and discover that reading is really not that bad! And when you get a chance, I would love for you to "read" more about Positive-Strides.org on our website www.positive-strides.org to learn more about our mission and how you might be able to help an injured athlete get through some tough times and maybe even read a book or two!

Part 1

Field Goals from Literacy Leaders

Letter from Kathryn Starke, Urban Literacy Specialist

Dear Readers,

As an urban literacy specialist and former classroom teacher in Title I inner city elementary schools, I'm so glad you have added Tackle Reading to your list of resources. In my position, I currently travel to urban elementary schools nationwide to motivate children, support parents, and inspire educators to love literacy. I train teachers on how to provide quality reading instruction for all children and help turn failing schools to fully accredited in one year. This book is a collection of stories and lessons for readers of all ages. Each entry has been coded with a C (children), P (parents), or E (educators) in the table of contents to determine the best way to implement the selection based on the subject matter. We have stories and activities that elementary-aged children can complete and read independently. We also encourage parents and teachers to read many of these inspirational stories to children. Finally, we have tips for parents and educators as well as lessons and reproducible materials that can be implemented in the home, classroom, or school community.

I am honored to have NFL players, literacy leaders, authors, celebrities, nonprofit organizations, and fellow teachers write their own original pieces for Tackle Reading. These individuals are dedicated to making a difference in reading education for children throughout the country. The USA ranks #24th in literacy. Research shows children who do not read on grade level by the time they are 9-years-old are more likely to fail and even drop out of school. National reading tests show that while 66% of our 9-year-olds read below grade level, 80% of 9-year-olds from low-income schools read below grade level. Thiry-two million adults, 14% of our population, can't read. What's more shocking is that we have not moved the needle in the past ten years. We can change these statistics today when we tackle reading together. In addition to this resource, we are launching the Tackle Reading tour, which will allow me to provide professional development for teachers and speaking engagements for parents, organizations, and businesses. We want to create a community of readers in every single city. I look forward to working with you! Thank you for you all do to provide quality reading instruction for all children. Let's #TackleReading today!

Sincerely,

Kathryn C. Starke

www.creativemindspublications.com
Facebook.com/creativemindspublications.com
Twitter.com/KathrynStarke
Instagram.com/KathrynStarke
Pinterest.com/KathrynStarke

Embrace the Dream
by Leigh DeFreitas

Reach out & read---
Embrace the dream
that books can change a life;
Since often journeys in this world
come wrapped and mapped with strife.

Take time & share---
Some words of hope
through stories of all kind;
Authors past and current pens
can stretch and mold a mind.

Set goals & soar---
To heights beyond
your greatest possible desire;
Help others to believe they can
read books that will inspire.

Decide & act---
Extend a hand
unlock the mystery;
Show how a book enriches life…
Make dreams reality.

Reach out & read---
Embrace the dream
That you can open the door;
The portal to a world so grand
where life brings so much more.

Believe that putting books into
little hands today
CAN, tomorrow, change a life
in such a special way.

Embrace the dream!

Leigh DeFreitas, *retired reading specialist*

Quick Tips for Struggling and Reluctant Readers

My name is Danny B., and I was a struggling and reluctant reader.

For most of my childhood I was ashamed. Ironically, working with struggling and reluctant readers has become my specialty. Can I let you in on a little secret? Four out of five of your struggling and reluctant readers are going to be boys.

Boys and girls are very different. Girls will read books about boys. Boys refuse to read most books about girls. In over 20 years of working with struggling and reluctant readers, as well as training thousands of teachers and parents, I have stumbled across a number of different strategies that work.

On the bookmarks that I pass out to attendees at my trainings, I provide the following quick tips to help struggling and reluctant readers:

1. Let children select whatever they want to read. A football card or menu is just as legitimate as a classic novel.
2. Find books related to movies, video games, comics, etc.
3. Read aloud to children…constantly. Try to read things that are well above the reading level of your children so they can get excited about the functions of reading for information.
4. Read in front of children. If children never see their parents reading for fun, it is a good bet that they will not read for fun.
5. Get children magazine and newspaper subscriptions.
6. Find shorter books with shorter chapters.
7. Sports and nonfiction rule. So do funny books. The more pictures, the better!
8. Reverse psychology: tell children that a book is too difficult for them to read.

9. Promote books with cool covers: dinosaurs, car crashes, cash, etc.
10. Keep boys' interests in mind. Little Women is great, but if you want a boy to be interested in it, you might add "diarrhea" or "vomit" to the title.

Remember to arm yourself with plenty of weapons of mass instruction, as what works for one student does not necessarily work for another. What is most critical is to always make reading fun. It does not matter what you read; what matters most is how much you read. Following the interests of the child is the secret to reading success, and introducing a love of reading to children is one of the most rewarding experiences I've ever known.

The son of a librarian, Dr. Danny Brassell (www.dannybrassell.com) grew up hating reading. Ironically, he is now considered "America's Leading Reading Ambassador." Speaking to over 100 audiences of schools, businesses and associations worldwide each year, Danny's mission is to celebrate the work of educators and inspire them to constantly improve their leadership skills.

A Week's Worth of Literacy Tips in Guided Reading

by Dr. Jan Richardson

Tip #1

I see guided reading fitting comfortably into the Common Core paradigm. Guided reading provides the opportunity to differentiate instruction for students who are experiencing difficulty applying the standard independently or for advanced readers who need to be challenged. Teachers could model the Common Core and state standards during whole-group instruction using grade-level text. Then, if teachers weave that same standard into a guided reading lesson, students would be able to practice the standard on a slightly challenging text with some teacher scaffolding.

Tip #2

Scaffolding

Guided reading provides the opportunity for teachers to assess student processing, differentiate according to need, provide appropriate scaffolding and gradually release teacher support so the student becomes more independent. "Scaffolding (a critical component of guided reading) involves the provision of temporary supports that allow students to successfully accomplish a task that is too challenging for them to accomplish on their own" (Lipson & Wixson, 2010, Successful Approaches to RTI p. 35).

Tip #3

Strategy

"A strategy is an action a reader takes to solve a problem in the text. Emergent and early readers tend to be overt in their use of strategies. You will often see them look at the picture, reread, or try to sound out a word. Transitional readers may be hesitant to try an unknown word. If a student appeals for help, always say, 'I want you to try.' You will learn more about a student's reading process if the student makes an attempt and is incorrect. Analyzing a student's strategies will help you to decide how to prompt the student during guided reading lessons." (Richardson, J. 2009. Next Step in Guided Reading, p. 43).

Tip #4
Individual Conferences

It is impossible to know for certain that students are reading and understanding their self-selected books, but one way to monitor this is through individual conferences. Try to meet with each student about once a week to discuss his or her independent reading. You can further monitor their understanding by asking students to draw or write about their reading in a readers' notebook.

Tip #5
Selecting an Emergent Text

How do you select a text for emergent readers who don't know any sight words? Choose a text with one line of print and a repetitive pattern. Make sure most of the pictures contain familiar concepts. After you have each child discuss one of the pictures, rehearse the structure by reading the first page together. Then let the students read the rest of the book independently while you prompt them to match 1:1 and check the picture. If students get stuck on a sight word, you could ask them to show you the word on that page and then reread the sentence. After reading you'll have the opportunity to teach them their first sight word.

Tip #6
Selecting Informational Texts for Guided Reading

Nonfiction books are great for guided reading. Children are attracted by the vivid photographs and motivated by their quest to know about real things. Select books that match your students' interests and have rich text features. Consider the level range of your readers. As a general rule of thumb, I select nonfiction texts one level below the group's instructional level. The book should offer some challenges so that students will have to use strategies, but it should be easy enough to allow them to experience success.

Tip #7

When a Guided Reading Lesson Flops

Have you ever taught a guided reading lesson that didn't go well? I certainly have. It's embarrassing, especially when you are demonstrating in front of a group of teachers. Most of the time the lesson flops because the text is too difficult. What do I do? Sometimes we'll read a few pages together and talk about the book. Other times I just apologize for making the wrong choice and choose a more appropriate book next time.

Jan Richardson, Ph.D., *is a literacy consultant and author who earned her Ph.D. studying struggling readers. She has been a classroom teacher, reading specialist, Reading Recovery® teacher leader, and staff developer. Her book, The Next Step in Guided Reading and DVD and Guide, Next Step Guided Reading in Action, provide teachers with practical suggestions and lesson plans for increasing the power and impact of guided reading. Visit www.janrichardsonguidedreading.com for more information.*

Experiential Learning:
Schoolwide Innovative Approaches to Spotlight Literacy

by Grace Nall

"The best and most memorable things in the world cannot be seen or even touched — they must be felt with the heart."
— Helen Keller

Imagine the possibilities when what is learned in a classroom of a Title I public elementary school is applied in a real-life community effort. According to Dr. David Kolb, experiential learning "is the process whereby knowledge is created through the transformation of experience." Life-long learning experiences involve a process of interpreting an existing experience. When we reflect on the experience, we can modify or give rise to a new idea. These reflections are tested in future situations to result in new learning experiences.

With many public schools affected by continuing budget cuts and education reform, the challenge to find effective and innovative learning approaches for students puzzles many teachers. Despite the obstacles, teachers are finding opportunities to make a positive impact on students' learning. I call these opportunities "teaching moments." The "teaching moments" take students on an experiential learning journey through hands-on participation.

The school where I teach is near a military base and students come from many multicultural backgrounds. Nearly 85% of our Grades K-5 student population is enrolled in free and/or reduced lunch programs. Research has shown a correlation between proper nutrition and cognitive ability in children. The students come from low-income households where multigenerational families live together. Quality time for academic support or help with student homework is limited when both parents work late hours. Parents and community involvement are low. All of this poses great learning challenges that teachers must overcome.

The good news is that Title I schools have funds for supplemental instruction or after-school enrichment academic opportunities to close the learning achievement gap. Experiential learning opportunities provide a collaborative meaningful and purposeful planning to enrich the learning experiences for students. After-school tutoring in reading and writing reinforces language arts skills. As students gain confidence in social skills, this helps them learn faster through active engagement.

As a National Board Certified Teacher passionate about literacy, I sought ways to bring fun and education into an after-school enrichment "tutoring" academy for fourth and fifth graders by coordinating author visits during the National Education Association's (NEA) Read Across America themed activities.

In 2008, author Caroline Hatton asked if I could create a teacher resource guide for her book, The Night Olympic Team: Fighting to Keep Drugs Out of the Games, to use in the classroom. Our fundraising efforts were limited. No author had ever visited the Title I school. Hatton had to be the first.

Together with school colleagues and a "think-outside-the-box" approach, we took this opportunity to involve and engage the staff, students, parents, and community. Hatton was also a scientist who worked at the UCLA Olympic laboratory testing athletes. The 2008 Summer Olympics in China were just beginning and provided a rich opportunity to create a parallel timely experiential learning component. The school brought in a personal trainer and built a mock Olympic course for the students to see what training was like for Olympians.

This attracted local media attention, which created valuable exposure for a school in need of educational funds. Hatton talked about her book at the author school assembly and book signing at a nearby Barnes and Noble book store. This motivated the students to want to read her book and it created a greater interest in literacy.

Since then, our school's NEA Read Across America activities have featured children's book authors Bruce Hale, Salina Yoon,

Marcia Berneger, Shannon Hale, Suzanne Santillan, Matthew Ward, and many others. The Parent-Teacher Organization (PTO) became more involved in the process by helping develop a partnership with Barnes and Noble, which led to a fund-raising event that brought more books into our classroom. In 2013, our school received a $4,200 donation from City National Bank to purchase more than 800 books from Barnes and Noble Booksellers, a gift from the community through its Holiday Book Drive. During the same year, an after-school enrichment tutoring "club" called the Authors, Illustrators, and Journalists (AIJ) Academy was formed to include fourth and fifth students in learning about reading and writing beyond the classroom experience. In 2014, a NEA "Read Across America" grant helped our school acquire more books. The AIJ students created a simulated newscast as a way of thanking NEA Read Across America and its sponsor Renaissance Dental. The AIJ Academy 45News was produced by a local award-winning broadcast journalist and entrepreneur, Phoebe Chongchua, and her company ThinkLikeAJournalist. com. Students applied what they learned in the classroom using experiential learning. They wrote news scripts and a commercial, as well as interviewed authors for news reports. See the newscast: https://www.youtube.com/watch?v=qomVu1XqbOM

We discovered that there is no better way to teach students about writing, journalism, broadcasting, marketing, and technology than with a student-run, written, and produced TV Newscast. As a former local journalist, my experiences helped to serve as a mentor to the students in creating an annual Read Across America newsletter. The result of the newscast was increased enrollment in the program; it nearly tripled, attracting 33 students in 2015.

Every time students have that "aha" moment when they are transformed through the art of experiential learning, it is, for me, like finding gems in a treasure chest. But the real gift is not only the students' educational gain but also the inspiration that has motivated the staff. The students came from a variety of learning styles and multicultural backgrounds. Their diverse interests in learning sparked excitement among all the academy members.

Experiential learning has been connected to community-based research, learning styles, academic service learning, the connected classroom, problem-based learning, real-world simulations, and creative expression. With experiential learning, the concept of teachers and students learning from each other can nurture a positive collaborative environment.

In 2016, our school added a leadership initiative based on Stephen Covey's Leader in Me and Sean Covey's The 7 Habits of Happy Kids. The Read Across America activities included a finale resulting in a "Community of Leaders as Readers" Event. Many community leaders, including two NFL San Diego Chargers Wide Receivers, visited our school to read to students. The school-wide effort and the PTO helped to make the reading event a memorable one and prompted coverage by CBS Channel 8 KFMB –TV in San Diego, CA.

The Four Stages of Experiential Learning

Source: Dr. David Kolb

1. Experience: Students are involved in a learning experience.

2. Reflection: Students observe and reflect on the experience.

3. Conceptualize: Students analyze and form abstract concepts and conclusions from the experience.

4. Test: How does this work in future situations and new experiences for students?

Experiential learning takes us on a life-long journey where students can enter the cycle at any stage and follow through a logical sequence. It is a "think-outside-of-the-box" method to enhance education. As philosopher John Dewey says, learning naturally occurs through active involvement that demands critical thinking skills. "We do not learn from experience... we learn from reflecting on experience."

Grace Nall, National Board Certified Teacher, Educational Consultant
Website: http://www.teachingseasons.com/

Reading Counts: The Very Best Children's Books to Explore Mathematics: A Baker's Dozen
Dr. Jeannine R. Perry

Story has always been a conduit to explain and instruct because it takes specialized concepts and ideas and embeds them in familiar, real-world situations so we can better understand and make connections. All too often, story is only associated with the "literary" world of letters and words in the make-believe realms of adventure, romance, fantasy, tragedy, and comedy. However, story told through a mathematical lens helps us celebrate the language and beauty of mathematics, see the role it plays in our daily lives, and better understand what it's like to see the world through a mathematical perspective. Unfortunately, exposure to mathematics in schools has traditionally been through textbooks, flashcards, and workbooks. It is isolated and disconnected from its purpose so the symbols used to communicate mathematical concepts, thoughts, and ideas are never fully integrated. Whitin and Wilde (1995) state, "right answers in a textbook are not synonymous with understanding in the real world; unless learners have stories to tell about mathematical concepts, they have no understanding of those concepts." Artfully written children's books that provide meaningful contexts for mathematical concepts not only help to teach those concepts but show how math is part of our human story and experience.

There are hundreds of children's books that teach mathematical concepts. Some are far more didactic than others---written to instruct rather than experience. While some of these are interesting and effective, others are no more than a textbook or a word problem disguised as a story. There are, however, some truly outstanding authors and illustrators whose work celebrates math as a language and as an integral part of the human experience. These authors both explain and play with mathematics as part of a real story—a story with which the reader can easily identify. After nearly three decades of collecting, sharing, and teaching with children's books that contain mathematical concepts, I would like to recommend some absolute treasures everyone should read and all teachers should include in their libraries and mathematics instruction. These books link mathematics to art, poetry, nature, music, and daily life in memorable ways. They help those of us who do not see the world through a mathematical lens naturally understand those who do. They use language artfully while explaining and exploring mathematics.

As with all good books, these should be read and viewed (illustrations are as important as text in picture books) for enjoyment above all else and then returned to and explored for their many nuances—especially the mathematical ones.

The Math Curse
Jon Scieszka and illustrator Lane Smith

From the book jacket to the dedication this hilarious, complex book is filled with math in ways only mathematicians can appreciate--which is the point! It begins with, "On Monday in math class Mrs. Fibonacci says, 'you know, you can think of almost everything as a math problem.' On Tuesday I start having problems." The main character then goes through the next day seeing the world through mathematical eyes and encountering one problem after another because, as he concludes, he has been cursed to do so. However, the real world is never left out as he struggles through breakfast, the bus ride, English, and sharing the class birthday treat when there isn't enough to go around. Best of all, problems are not always solved with traditional mathematical methods and questions and answers reflect that there are other aspects to life beyond mathematics.

How Many Snails: A Counting Book
Each Orange Had 8 Slices: A Counting Book
Paul Giganti and illustrator Donald Crews

These are not ordinary counting books! The patterned language, attention to attributes, and use of environmental context are instructional but also serve as models for individual writing and mathematical problem solving.

How Many Snails focuses on counting attributes as the speaker shares a variety of places she has visited and things she has seen there:

I went walking to the meadow and I wondered:
How many flowers were there?
How many flowers were yellow?
How many flowers were yellow with black centers?

Writers enjoy figuring out the language pattern, selecting their own favorite place to go and special thing to see, and then figuring out two attributes to complete the sequence. Here is the template for modeled writing:

I went (action verb) to the (location) and I wondered:
How many (main object) were there?
How many (main object) were (attribute 1)?
How many (main object) were (attribute 1) with/and had (attribute 2)?

In Each Orange Had 8 slices, Giganti plays with multiplication using a similar language pattern. On my way to the playground I saw 3 red flowers.

Each red flower had 6 pretty petals.
Each petal had 2 tiny black bugs.
How many red flowers were there?
How many pretty petals were there?
How many tiny black bugs were there in all?

This one is a bit more complex as a writing model, but lots of discussion and practice leads to clear understanding and fantastic ideas as writers come up with their own versions. Here is the template for modeled writing:

On my way to (location) I saw (adjective) (# less than 10) (object 1).
Each (object 1) had (#) (attribute/object 2)
Each (attribute/object 2) had (#) (attribute/object 3).
How many (object 1) were there?
How many (attribute/object 2) were there?
How many (attribute/object 3) were there in all?

Counting on Frank
Rod Clement

This humorous story celebrates those who think differently; who imagine, wonder, experiment, and ask questions. It features a boy and his dog estimating, measuring, comparing, and hypothesizing. It begins with: "My dad says, 'You have a brain. Use it!' So I do. I sit down and fill my notebook with facts. Did you know that the average ball-point pen draws a line seven thousand feet long before the ink runs out? My parents consider this fact to be a bit childish, but I'm sure the pen company would like to know." The main character of this story helps the reader see the world through his curious and mathematical eyes–and it is a very different world!

The primary focus of this story is estimation, however, in addition to "the facts" this story puts mathematics into real-world context by dealing with the realities of life and the implications of mathematical hypotheses. For example, he imagines and estimates how large he'd be if he grew as fast as a tree, but wonders where he would find shoes to fit? Or, he calculates what size he would be if he put on every piece of clothing in his closet, but is pretty sure he could never sit down with so many clothes on.

10 Black Dots
Donald Crews

This simple, yet extraordinary book, explores shape in an environmental and experiential context along with counting from 1-10. It encourages us to view the world through the lens of geometry and number through rhythmic language.

1 dot can make a sun…or a moon when day is done.
2 dots can make the eyes of a fox…or the eyes of keys that open locks.

Self adhesive dots are inexpensive and easy to use for writers to create their own stories once they begin taking notice of shapes and numbers in the world around them. Why limit your writing to dots? How about squares or triangles?

Arthur's Funny Money
Lillian Hoban

This early reader chapter book has been around a long time, but it is one of the best ways to see real-world economics in action—and the special relationship of a big brother and his little sister. Older brother Arthur wants to buy a T-shirt and matching cap for his Frisbee team but he doesn't have enough money. He and younger sister Violet, being excellent entrepreneurs, decide to wash bikes to raise funds. Through the ups and downs of Arthur's business the economic concepts of needs and wants, opportunity cost, scarcity, goods and services, barter, money, and marketing are combined with lots of adding, subtracting, multiplying, and dividing and then mixed in with friendship, pets who eat soap, miscommunication, and the usual tensions and reconciliations between siblings. There are plenty of opportunities to do calculations, there's a tricky word problem, and of course discussion and extension of all the economic concepts that frame this story. Role play, readers' theater, or acting out scenes from the story are all great ways to explore and extend meaning.

The Math Wiz
Betsy Duffey

This is not a picture book, but it's a must read because it features a boy who thinks mathematically and struggles with one big problem…the P.E. Problem. Marty Malone sees everything through mathematical eyes. Marty observes and interprets the world in the form of problems and uses mathematical notation to express those problems. For example, Marty notices his baby brother is BABY + BOTTLE = QUIET BABY and starts wondering BABY – BOTTLE = ??? When he solves for ??? he finds the answer is WAAAAA!!! In third grade, Marty discovers a new problem. Math Wiz + P.E. = Misery. Marty isn't the best at P.E. and he doesn't know how to solve this problem. It just doesn't fit the mathematical world he is so comfortable in. For individuals who interpret the world like Marty, it's important that they see they are not alone. Readers will enjoy converting sentences and ideas into mathematical notations like Marty does throughout the book, integrating some of those challenging symbols (like greater than and less than) into real, daily experiences.

Only One
Marc Harshman and illustrator Barbara Garrison

This creative book explores how we combine single things like seeds or eggs or bees into one collective like a pumpkin or dozen or hive. It begins with "There may be a million stars, but there is only one sky" and ends with "But the best thing of all is that there is only one me and there is only one you." This book encourages us to see the world in different ways—wholes and parts—and think about how we use language to describe what we see. See how many more examples you can come up with modeled after the ones in this book.

Zin! Zin! Zin! a Violin
Lloyd Moss and illustrator Marjorie Priceman

Another story that focuses on the language of grouping, this begins: "With mournful moan and silken tone, itself alone comes ONE TROMBONE. Gliding, sliding, high notes go low; ONE TROMBONE is playing solo. Next, a TRUMPET comes along, and sings and stings its swinging song. It joins TROMBONE, no more alone, and ONE and TWO-O, they're a DUO." Sound words, rhyme, rhythmical language, and the unique character of different musical instruments blend with counting and grouping to celebrate math, music, and words. The illustrations are as rhythmical as the text and font size, and shape is used to further enhance the meaning conveyed.

Pigs Will Be Pigs
Amy Axelrod and illustrator Sharon McGinley-Nally

This is by far the best in a series of books featuring the lovable Pig family because the story is one most families have experienced. While this book was clearly designed to teach mathematical concepts, they are an integral part of a real experience embedded in humor and delightful language.

When the Pigs get hungry and find they have no snacks and no money (because mom didn't get to the bank) they "Hunt for Money!" throughout their house. As they find various combinations of coins and even some bills, it's fun to try to keep track of how much they have. But the fun doesn't stop there. Once they've found enough, the family takes a trip to the Enchanted Enchilada where they order from the menu (included in the book) and then need to see if they can afford their meal. Writers will have great fun coming up with their own money hunt, special restaurant, and menu when they use this book as a model to write their own story. Lots of counting and calculating will go in to the writing as well.

One Hundred Hungry Ants
Elinor Pinczes and illustrator Bonnie MacKain

This story follows the exploits of a little ant and all his fellow ants on their way to raid a picnic. The language is beautiful, the story is funny, and the math is clearly integral to the lives of the ants. In this story, a single line of 100 ants changes to a double line of 50, then 4 lines of 25, 5 lines of 20 and finally 10 lines of 10. But while the ants were "racing here and there, up, down and to and fro" to form their rows, the reader sees various forest creatures carrying picnic items in the opposite direction. Of course by the time the ants arrive, there are "no more yummies for their rumbling tummies" and "ninety-nine ants were swarming from each and every row, in hot pursuit of one little ant who quickly turned to go." Don't miss the companion book A Remainder of One, which explores what happens when you don't have an even number to make rows!

The Doorbell Rang
Pat Hutchins

This may have been one of the very first books recognized for its mathematical value but it remains a beautiful story about sharing, family, and community. Two children begin by sharing a dozen cookies, but before they can eat them the doorbell rings and two neighbors come in resulting in a redistribution of cookies. Of course, division is the mathematical concept behind this story, but it is embedded as sharing, not explicitly referred to as division. More and more friends and family come over until everyone has just one cookie...and then the doorbell rings again... Acting this story out promotes discussion and interaction with the mathematical concept and often results in extensions into fractions and problem solving-- but more importantly discussions about sharing and caring.

Alexander, Who Used to Be Rich Last Sunday
Judith Viorst

"It isn't fair that my brother Anthony has two dollars and three quarters and one dime and seven nickels and eighteen pennies. It isn't fair that my brother Nicholas has one dollar and two quarters and five dimes and five nickels and thirteen pennies. It isn't fair because what I've got is…bus tokens." While it's hard to resist trying to add up those tempting numbers of coins and while there is a clear portion of the story devoted to adding and subtracting money, this is still first and foremost a story. It's a story about a little boy who fights with his brothers, can't pass up a yard sale, loves the money his grandparents bring when they visit, and can't seem to hang onto it no matter how hard he tries. While some readers may need background information about bus tokens, everyone can identify with Alexander, who used to be rich but isn't anymore.

Measuring Penny
Loreen Leedy

While this book was clearly written with the intent of teaching a wide span of measurement concepts, it was put in the context of a beloved pet, Penny the dog, making it both memorable and remarkable. The main character, Lisa, is given a school assignment to measure something in several different ways. She decides to measure her dog and explores standard and nonstandard measures, height, width, weight, length, volume, temperature, time, cost and…most importantly…value. The story prompts the reader to see things through a measurement lens and writers can explore measuring their own choice of "something" from bricks to houses to stuffed animals.

Whitin, D. and Wilde, S. (1995). *It's the Story that Counts: More Children's Books for Mathematical Learning, K-6. Portsmouth, NH: Heinemann Publishers.*

Dr. Jeannine R. Perry
Associate Professor: Education-Reading, Learning & Literacy
Longwood University
Dean, College of Graduate & Professional Studies
Longwood University

Reading Reflection at Home

*The following questions can be used with any story to increase oral language skills and comprehension!

1. What do you think this story will be about? Use your picture clues to help.
2. Who is in this story? Describe the characters.
3. What's happening in this story? What's the big idea?
4. When does this story take place?
5. Where does this story take place?
6. What is the problem in this story? How do you think it will be solved?
7. What does this story make you think about?
8. What is the most important part of this story? Why?
9. What is your favorite part of the story? Why?
10. Would you recommend this story to a friend? Why or why not?

*These questions can be asked through conversation or the child can practice writing skills by answering one or two questions at a time in a journal.

*Research shows that reading at least 20 minutes a night helps a child perform better in school. Pick a time and place that works for your family.

Reading Clouds

by Kathryn Starke

When you tell children to read something, they follow your directions perfectly. They read the words on the page. They spend their energy decoding the sounds of every single word in each line in text. After they finish reading, you start to ask questions about the passage and they look at you with blank stares. If you recall, you told them simply to read. When we want our boys and girls to be able to engage in conversation and inquiry, we have to teach them. We also have to explicitly explain to them we want them to read and think until they do it naturally. The following pages are the reading clouds I created and displayed in my classroom to encourage my students to think throughout the entire reading process. We used these reading strategies in whole group, small group, during independent reading, and during reading tests until it was a reading habit. You will see Reading Expert bookmarks in Part 7 of this book that put the strategies in a natural order for the children to follow before, during, and after reading.

- ➤ Predict-make a prediction based on the title alone or the title and pictures (no words allowed).
- ➤ Picture Clues-use graphics and pictures to add meaning to reading.
- ➤ Make Connections-see if children have background knowledge to the text before reading to determine if you need to teach more about the topic/theme before reading; make connections again after reading to see if the text reminded them of something.
- ➤ Question (I, S, T) - ask and answer questions; some questions will be I know questions like a connection

question or a word analysis question (e.g., which word on page one has the same sound as cake?) Many questions will be Story questions, in which the answer is directly in the text. Finally, you will have Thinking questions. With these, prompt the children to use clues in the text (inference and critical skills) to answer the question.

➤ Read-exactly what you mean (often focus is on accuracy).

➤ Reread and Think-gives the children the opportunity to reread with fluency to focus more comprehension.

➤ Making Sense-clarify meaning of questions and statements to make sure there is full understanding.

➤ Prove Your Work-just like detectives have to prove their cases with evidence, readers have to prove their thinking and answers with evidence from the text.

Predict

Picture Clues

Questions I, S, T

Read!

Make Connections

Reread and Think

Making Sense

Part 2

Reading Passes

On the Ground with Tennessee Teachers:
Three Things We Learned from These Amazing Educators

by James Walter Doyle

I went to Tennessee to connect with teachers and learn how DonorsChoose.org can help them. What I got was an inspiring sense of community... and one phenomenal haircut. As part of my DonorsChoose.org teacher outreach work. I travel to different parts of the country to see what's happening on the ground. Recently, as part of a research grant from 100kin10, I found myself on a road trip from Nashville to Memphis—meeting educators and partner organizations, listening to their stories, and helping teachers post their first projects on our site.

Many of our country's teachers share common characteristics—dedication, creativity, and compassion—but every teacher also has unique strengths and concerns. It would be wrong of me to assume that my experiences teaching in Harlem are the same as those of, for example, teachers in rural Clarkson, Tennessee.

Here are just a few of the things I learned from the communities I visited in Nashville, Memphis, and the places in between.

It takes a village. Despite sometimes long distances between students, teachers, and their schools, the towns I visited were tight-knit. As a result, teachers are eager to share with their communities the exciting things their students are doing.

Posting projects on our site is just one way for them to do this and gain support—whether emotional or monetary. Their view of DonorsChoose.org as an opportunity to celebrate their students was inspiring and showcases how their communities embody the maxim: "It takes a village to raise a child."

We can always do more. We're always looking for new ways to help educators, and never has it been more clear to me that we should continue to do so than on this trip. Many of the teachers I met mentioned their students' need for basic, life-essential items. As one educator said:

"I know we should be thinking about nicer books or a carpet like you said as examples. But I don't spend my money on that. I am spending my money on socks for kids in the winter and yogurt cups for breakfast."

At DonorsChoose.org, we recently launched a small pilot for teachers to request these types of items. I was excited to share this news, but these conversations also reminded me that we should never stop exploring new options for our teachers.

Generosity begets generosity. The teachers I met had a "pay it forward" mindset, always looking for ways to help their students, coworkers, and community. Within minutes of posting their first project, teachers asked how they could spread the word to their colleagues. Instead of asking about minimums for thank you packages, one teacher asked if there was a "maximum number of cards… and is it possible to send a gift basket?"

This "pay it forward" attitude extends beyond the classroom for these educators. One teacher even insisted that I go to her husband's barbershop across the street from school for a free haircut.

It was the best I ever received.

———————

DonorsChoose.org has been helping teachers and students since 2000, and makes it easy for anyone to help a classroom in need. For example, DonorsChoose.org has helped 150,000 classrooms build a new classroom library. Public school teachers from every corner of America create classroom project requests, and you can give any amount to the project that inspires you. Outside of DonorsChoose.org, Walter is the founder and CEO of Kids N Culture. This small charity gives low-income students an opportunity to learn through experience while traveling abroad for the first time.

Doctors Prescribing Books Across America

by Susan Rockwell

Once Upon A Time…

There were nice doctors who took care of children everyday. Every check up, from the time the babies were little, the doctors checked their ears, heart, gave immunizations and also gave each a brand new book!

The doctors told Moms and Dads to read aloud as often as they could. The doctors taught other nice younger doctors to do the same, and THEY taught others and so on and so on…and that was the beginning of the national early childhood education program called Reach Out and Read (ROR).

THE END

Actually, a simple story began a 27-year-old intervention facilitated through the loving hands of pediatricians in their practices across the country. Today, 20.000 medical providers across the country give 4.5 million children 6 million books at check ups every year.

The prescription works because the medical providers sit at the heart. The pediatricians and nurses that practice ROR in their clinic are as unique as the model. Each comes to this practice with a story of his or her own. For instance,

- Dr. Boone was a child of a teenage pregnancy, and was raised by a foster parent. They did not have running water but thanks to her foster mother, she had books, and she quickly developed a love of reading. Books opened up new worlds for Dr. Boone and she was taught to share her passion for reading with others, a lesson she took to heart. Dr. Boone remembers, "We were poor but I could travel all over the world in a book. I could be anyone I wanted to be."

- Dr. Addie Briggs has murals painted on each exam room wall. In the teenage exam room, there is a painting of a university with graduates extending their arms as they throw their hats in the air. It is graduation day! She wants her patients to see themselves in those students.

- Dr. Melaney Caldwell understands that as an African American female physician, she is a role model for many of her patients. Two young female patients asked her how she became a doctor and she told them. I read books and I worked hard in school. Both of these girls are enrolled in med school today.

- Dr. Joyce Whitaker attended medical school and performed her residency in other cities while always intending to return to her hometown to treat children in her community. She dedicates her efforts to changing the tide of illiteracy and she now sees children and grandchildren of some of her first pediatric patients having encouraged multigenerations of a family to read together.

- How often does one see a mother and son, Dr. Lillian Bennett and Dr. Richard Bennett, both pediatricians, working side by side treating their patients holistically prescribing medicine AND books, feeding healthy minds as well as healthy bodies?

Another compelling component are the children and families that receive Reach Out and Read. ROR families are reported to read four to eight times more than those that do not receive an ROR prescription.

- How about the young five-year-old boy whose Mom made it home on the bus only to discover that they had left their book at the pediatric office. The little boy remained bereft until they returned on the bus to retrieve the book.

- The excitement of a group of families and staff as they watch the two-year-old boy who runs with glee throughout the waiting room because he has just received a new book of his very own from his pediatrician.

- Six years ago, there is a Dad, recently paroled, who patiently waits with his baby girl to see the doctor where they receive their ROR intervention. Today, his little girl is the best reader in her fourth-grade class.

- A family celebrates for their 21-year-old son as he graduates from college as the first in the family. Dad will continue to work three jobs to ensure that younger sister will also have the same opportunity.

- The simple act of a young boy sitting on his mother's lap with a book in hand announcing, "Mom, I am reading" as they await their appointment with a ROR doctor.

Emphasizing the first five years of life, which is the critical window for learning, ROR focuses on the opportunity to address children during this rapid time of brain development. Many children, especially those from low-income families, are not read to from birth and grow up with significantly less exposure to language and basic literacy skills.

Research shows that children who enter school on track are more likely to reach their full educational, social, and life potential which means we will begin to move the literacy needle in a positive direction. ROR, as part of the national initiative to address the illiteracy issue, will continue to build on the unique relationship between parents and medical professionals to develop the essential literacy skills that prepare children for educational success and beyond.

Susan Rockwell is the director of Reach Out and Read Virginia/DC.

Breaking the Cycle

by Gary Anderson

It's an all-too familiar cycle. By upper elementary and middle school, many urban students (and a fair number of suburban students as well) have tuned out to reading. They scuffle through high school and emerge, if they're lucky, with a diploma. But their low literacy skills condemn them to a life of low-paying, dead-end jobs. Without a role model for reading, their children eventually slide out of the education process as well. And the cycle perpetuates itself across generations.

There's a surprisingly simple way to help break the low literacy/poverty cycle. We need to harness the power of parents to help kids build the reading habit. Increasing numbers of school leaders are discovering that a shared reading program called One District, One Book can engage families throughout their school or district in building children's reading skills. The program engages all elementary families in a school or district by having them read a chapter a night of the same children's book, and it is especially effective in reaching families that do not typically get involved in school activities.

"We all talk about needing more parent engagement, but most educators struggle with how to get parents engaged," said José Parra, superintendent of the Irving Independent School District in Texas. "Parents want to be helpful. We just have to show them how. The One District, One Book program has given us a mechanism to show parents how they can work with their kids and help, and have it also be an enjoyable experience."

According to a 2015 survey by Scholastic, more than half of children ages 0–5 (54%) are read aloud to at home 5–7 days a week. This declines to one in three kids ages 6–8 (34%) and one in six kids ages 9–11 (17%). Yet more than eight in ten children

(83%) across age groups say that they loved or liked being read aloud to—mainly because it was a special time with parents.

Conversely, parents realize the vital importance of reading skills for youngsters. More than seven out of ten parents of children ages 6-17 (71%) rank strong reading skills as the most important skill a child should have (and 54% of kids agree). Furthermore, three out of four parents (75%) wish their children would read more books for fun.

So, how do we build on this inherent interest in reading and being read to? We need a shift in family culture to include time for reading. We need a shift in children's behavior away from screen time to spending more time reading for pleasure as a family. We need a shift in parents' behavior away from being "nagging homework tutors" to becoming literacy leaders in the home. We need a shift in schools and communities to recognize that rather than holding schools 100% responsible for developing children as readers we need to involve families and the community.

Across the United States, schools and districts—and even entire states—are discovering the power of a shared reading experience to bring communities together around reading. Through the One District, One Book and One School, One Book programs, literally millions of elementary families have been swept into the reading habit by reading the same great children's book at the same time. The program continues to expand. Texas did a statewide Texas Reads One Book program in 2015 and 2016. New York State is getting ready to launch its own statewide initiative, and other states are exploring similar programs.

Imagine the power when reading becomes the hot topic of discussion in schools, in families, and often throughout the entire community as families read a chapter together each night at home and the school adds in other supporting activities. The program uses positive peer pressure to create momentum for reading. When everyone in a school or district is reading a book, no children or families want to be left out. And since EVERY FAMILY in participating schools or districts receives a copy of the book, everyone can be involved.

"The program brought in parents who normally don't participate," said Steve Anderson, superintendent of the Lake Hamilton School District in Arkansas. "We want to change the culture in this area to promote reading in the family."

Together, families discover the joys of sharing books such as Charlotte's Web, The One and Only Ivan, or the Humphrey series. And, as they read together over the course of a month, the reading habit starts to grow. Schools and districts that do two books a year discover a real shift in the reading culture among students—a shift that can show up in test scores as well.

For instance, schools in Northumberland, Virginia, saw passage rates on the statewide third-grade reading assessment increase by more than 30 percentage points after participating in the One District, One Book program. In Watertown, New York, which has been doing two books a year for several years, the percentage of elementary school families who reported that they read for pleasure every night rose from 8% to 57% between spring 2014 and fall 2015–an amazing testimonial to the power of building the reading habit.

The shift is massive when entire districts participate in a shared book program. Typically, 95% of all the elementary school families participate because everybody—including the haves and have nots—are involved. They do not want to be left out. In a district's overall budget, providing this powerful shared book experience through the One District, One Book program can be accomplished at a very reasonable cost, and it provides a strong complement to the schools' overall literacy programs. In fact, in an era when budget cutting remains the norm, Superintendent David Pennington of Ponca City Public Schools in Oklahoma said, "This is the last program we would ever cut."

"It's really great to have everyone talking about the same book," noted Superintendent Ricardo López of Mission Consolidated Independent School District in Texas. "What we are trying to do is transform the community through literacy."

Our schools are excellent, but they cannot do it alone. They need to work together with all the families who have children in the schools. This happens in communities that participate in the One District, One Book program because everyone is literally on the same page. Districts that participate over a period of several years end up building a community of readers. It's a win-win-win for families, for schools, and for communities.

Gary Anderson is the founder of the nonprofit organization Read to Them, which runs the One District, One Book and One School, One Book programs. Learn more at www.readtothem.org.

Richmond Reads More Books

by Gail Henshaw

"I Have A Dream" Foundation® – Richmond has championed reading as a cornerstone of our program since we began working with elementary school students in the City of Richmond, Virginia in 2007. We have brought guest readers to the classrooms, held novel studies after school, sponsored reading/book report incentive programs, brought visiting authors to the school, implemented and utilized Accelerated Reader (a web-based reading comprehension program), and given thousands of books to students to take home. We began work at one elementary school with one grade level and have slowly expanded to include the entire school, then multiple schools, then system-wide, and beyond. In total, "I Have A Dream" Richmond has distributed over 110,000 books!

Does this make a difference to anyone? We believe so, as evidenced by comments from the recipients of books for their home libraries:

> "Do I really get to keep this book at my house and not bring it back?"

> "I'm putting this where my little brother can't reach it!"

> "I know this is a book, but I'm going to take it home and wait until Christmas to unwrap it."

> "I have five books that you gave me [over the years], and I keep them by my bed and read them over and over again."

> "Can you bring me a book about cats?"

"Thank you very much for the book. It is the best gift I ever got."

"Hey! There's the book lady!"

Yes, reading initiatives do make a difference. In addition to giving students their own new, age-appropriate, subject-appropriate book, we have used other means to instill a love of reading. Assemblies have been a great way to build excitement. Hearing the students chant "Read More Books! Read More Books!" in order to call a mascot in to help distribute books has been an uplifting, memorable occasion for students, educators, and volunteers. For the competitive spirits, we have provided visual aids that chart each student's success and rewarded budding readers and authors with lunch in a limo.

Let's keep putting books in the hands of young people and providing creative, fun reading-related activities. Let's Tackle Reading and Read More Books together!

———————

Gail Henshaw
Sponsor,
"I Have A Dream" Foundation – Richmond, Virginia
http://ihaveadreamrichmond.org/

Knowledge Is Power...
But Sharing the Knowledge Is Compassionate

by Scott Graham

When I think about Coin Up, a mobile app that is destined to change the way people give to charity, I cannot help having to go back to my roots as a child. Education was heavily stressed to both my sister and I at a very young age. In particular, reading was an important element of our early developmental progress. I can remember being around ten years old during the summertime in sunny California; and sitting at our kitchen table having to read the newspaper and write a report on what I had learned from the various articles. I could hear the neighborhood kids outside playing and would always wonder why I had to read these "silly" articles that my parents assigned me when I'm not even in school right now.

As I became older, I began to understand the importance of that early foundation of reading. As my vocabulary increased, I became more confident to express my thoughts and opinions. It didn't matter if I were speaking to my peers or adults; I was able to stand my own ground without fear or hesitation. Beyond those initial memories, however, there is one key thing that stood out from my childhood as it relates to reading and it involves Christmas. I was very fortunate to have received many of the things that I wanted during the holidays. In addition to the abundance of toys and clothes that were given to us, we always received new books to read. There was a catch though when it came to the books. My parents always made us put a pile of books that we had finished reading and give them to kids that were less fortunate. It was their belief that the more knowledge you receive, the more powerful you become. With that power, comes the responsibility to share it by passing it along to others.

Then and more importantly now, I embrace the ability to take what I've learned from reading a variety of things (books, magazines, blogs) and passing that information along to others. My parents instilled in me that sharing your knowledge with others is one of the most compassionate things that someone could do. So remember, every time you read and continue to evolve as a human being, never forget to pass that knowledge onto others. It's one thing to possess something as powerful as knowledge, but it's selfless to share that knowledge with others.

Scott Graham *is the cofounder and chief technology officer of Coin Up, a mobile app that allows people to donate their spare change to causes they are passionate about, every time they make a purchase on their credit or debit card. He graduated from Fresno State University, where he played basketball under the leadership of legendary coach Jerry Tarkanian.*

Part 3

Touchdowns On and Off the Field from NFL Players

Voice of Victory

by Dion Foxx, M.ED

L ooking back at it all growing up was great. I can remember recess, lunch with my friends laughing, and learning new things in class. In order to learn new things you have to read about them. Reading can take you to new places and help you to imagine things that you have never seen before. I also know that reading may not be fun at times when you don't feel like doing it. Certain things may keep you from wanting to read. Being shy could be a reason because of a lack of confidence. Maybe you don't like how you sound when you read out loud. It could also be that you don't like not knowing all the words or that you may have problems sounding them out. Don't worry about that because it happens to all of us at one time or another.

I know because I can tell you a story about a kid I know that had those same things happen growing up. He had a hard time in elementary school when it came to being confident with his reading. His came from a stuttering problem. This was something that was an issue for a few years for him. This kid tried to read out loud in class sometimes, but he was worried about being laughed at by his classmates. He didn't want his friends to make fun of his stuttering problem. He went to speech classes to help work on the speech problem and to help with his confidence in reading with and in front of his classmates. It was easy for him to hide it or keep it a secret when he was playing with his friends and having regular conversation. This young man spent many of his elementary school years in speech classes to help his problem and gain confidence with his obstacle. He worked really hard at making sure he would never have to deal with this stuttering problem again. By the time this little guy made it to the fifth grade his stuttering problem was just about gone. He had gained a lot of confidence in reading books, talking to his friends, and more. He was also more confident with answering questions out loud in class for participation when asked. The tools that this young man learned helped him overcome and be victorious over his stuttering problem and become a better reader, more confident speaker, student, and person.

This young man learned valuable tools to make sure he continued to improve and stay victorious over this obstacle until it was no longer a problem at all. In fact, this young man went on to graduate from high school and earn a full scholarship to college to play athletics and obtain a degree. After graduating from college he was given the opportunity to play professional football in the NFL and CFL. After he retired, he pursued his next career in education and obtained a second Degree in Special Education so he could become a teacher and work with children with learning disabilities. He has been teaching for nine years and just recently went back to school where he graduated with his Masters of Education in Educational Leadership. This young man also helps out with promoting reading events for elementary school students, where he goes out and talks to students about the importance of reading to help visit and explore new places with your imagination. It is important to know how much reading can help with your vocabulary and learning new words by seeing and sounding them out. This young man has also had speaking engagements at universities, high schools, and special events showing that the years of reading and working on his vocabulary helped with his confidence, communication, and speaking skills.

Along the journey he has taught reading comprehension on the middle school level for a few years as well. Reading can do so many things for you and it all starts with just a little confidence and accepting help to get that victory so it can take you where you want to go in life. I still know this young man today. Overcoming his fears of reading and gaining confidence in himself really helped this young man be who he is today. That young man is ME, Dion Foxx. I overcame many obstacles and will continue to hurdle, climb, or bust through them, and you can too. I hope you enjoyed this story and it encourages you to read more, to better yourself, and to help you follow your dreams to be whatever you want to be in life. Remember to read because a good book can take you anywhere you want to go.

Dion L. Foxx (born June 11, in Richmond, Virginia) is a former American football linebacker in the National Football League. Dion Foxx played for the Miami Dolphins, the Washington Redskins, and went to camp with the Green Bay Packers. Foxx's playing career also included stints in the Canadian Football League, where he played for the Saskatchewan Roughriders and in the XFL with the Birmingham Bolts. Foxx began as a standout player at Meadowbrook High School in Richmond, Val. Foxx went on to become a dominant linebacker at James Madison University. In recent years, he has taught at the middle school and high school levels, and coaches high school football. Dion Foxx is also a member of Omega Psi Phi fraternity, Incorporated. Foxx is dedicated to his community and offers his services. He is affiliated with numerous charitable organizations where he gives his time for such causes.

Unleashing My Full Potential Through Reading

by Charles Johnson as told to Kathryn Starke

I grew up in a small town in the South called Hawkinsville, Georgia, which has less than 5,000 people. Everyone in a small town is very connected. I went to elementary, middle, and high school in Hawkinsville and have good memories of school, especially high school. Before my senior year, I was far enough ahead with my credits and classes that by my senior year, I only had to take gym and computer classes. This extra time during my senior year helped me prepare for playing football in college.

When I was little, I wanted to be a construction worker or a truck driver. My uncle was a truck driver in Hawkinsville and would take us on rides. I really didn't even think about playing professional football until I was in high school. I knew that playing sports in school would help me get out of the house and stay busy. I focused on my athletic ability, but, at the time, didn't put as much focus on my studies. In tenth grade, some college coaches started visiting me and looking at my transcripts, which at the time did not look very good, and were not reflective of my potential. This was the defining moment for me to start taking school more seriously. In my junior and senior years I got A's and B's and earned acceptance into the University of Georgia. I was a proud student-athlete for the Bulldogs for three seasons before being drafted by the Carolina Panthers.

As I look back, I sometimes wish I had focused on my academics earlier in life. I thought reading was pretty boring as a child. I remember just reading all of the Dr. Seuss books or any books made by Nickelodeon. (I loved watching Nickelodeon on TV.) In my town in rural Georgia, the library book fair was the only time to really get books. One of the coolest books I remember was the first ever Harry Potter book. I'm really into Greek mythology and wizardry. It's important to find books you are interested in. For me, I just needed to find a subject that appealed to me. We have to get kids hooked on reading early on, and we can do this by opening their eyes to the world of learning. There are so many subjects and areas of interest. Different topics relate to different kids. Today, I read to learn more and provide a love of reading to my own child.

Reading is part of practically every job that exists, even football. In fact, reading is a huge part of playing in the NFL. You have to read and understand all of the plays to get on the field. Outside of your job, you have to read what you like and what's important to you. I'm big on broadening my awareness on business management today. I started the Charles Johnson Foundation to help youth reach their full potential through athletics and education. We provide college scholarships to high school boys and girls every year to help them do great things. Find your passion, sports or something else, and start reading all about it today.

About Charles Johnson and the Charles Johnson Foundation

Charles Johnson is a native of Hawkinsville, Georgia, and a proud alumnus of Hawkinsville High School. After attending the University of Georgia where he starred at defensive end, Charles was drafted by the Carolina Panthers of the NFL in 2007 and has served as a captain of the team for three seasons.

Through nine professional seasons, Charles has received All-Pro recognition on the strength of 63.5 career sacks, placing him among the premier pass-rushers in the league. Charles ranks second on the Panthers' all-time sacks list. He helped Carolina win the NFC Championship and earn a spot in the 2016 Super Bowl.

In 2012, Charles' passion for philanthropy and loyalty to Middle Georgia led him to launch the Charles Johnson Foundation. A nonprofit organization, the Charles Johnson Foundation is dedicated to fulfilling a twofold mission:

- Providing opportunities for underserved youth to reach their full potential through athletic, recreational, and educational programs and initiatives; and

- Providing support for single African American mothers through proven programs and initiatives.

The Charles Johnson Foundation Sports Academy & Community Weekend is the flagship annual event for the Charles Johnson Foundation, combining his efforts to advance education with free sports clinics in football, basketball, tennis, dance, and cheer. Visit charlesjohnsonfoundation.org to learn more.

Football Mom

by Kendall Hall

When one thinks about a football player, a baseball player, or any other type of athlete, the mind goes right to performance on the field. Not many "fans" truly understand the long, hard, and sometimes very physical and emotional journey many successful athletes have been through to achieve greatness on that field. Many don't remember that before one was great, one had to start, and the classroom is not where many think the start began. But it did.

So many young men and women who are successful athletes, and I'm not talking about professionally, I'm speaking mostly of high school and college athletes, had to fight many battles off the field, and for so many of them it was in the classroom. You see, not just reading but learning in general can be a serious challenge for many of our young men and women. This challenge is sometimes mounted upon social and emotional challenges as well. Maybe a young man comes from a tough family, absentee parents, or is having to find ways to eat after a long day at school and practice. Many know that if he or she wants to have a better life, then he or she not only has to excel on the field but also in the classroom. Reading is the foundation of that success.

As the wife of a head football coach for 25 years, I have had the pleasure, but also experienced the pain, of watching young men listen, regardless of their circumstances, to peers, mentors, and coaches that surrounded them. I have watched so many succeed out of high school. They have done this because education came first, they knew it had to. I have had the pleasure of watching many of our young men sign division 1 scholarships and receive an education along with the opportunity to participate in college sports. Many have gone on to divisions 2 and 3 as well, hundreds over the years as a matter of fact. We have an NFL player in Kavell Conner, we have young men studying to be doctors, lawyers, and chemical engineers. We have a fighter pilot in the US Navy! But the ones that warm my heart the most, are the three young men who have returned from college to become teachers and mentors of young men, right where they began, in the halls of Manchester High School. And even more, they call me "mom." There is no better gift than that.

Kendall Hall is an elementary school teacher in Chesterfield County.

My Journey Through School

by Quinton Spain

School was not very important to me at a young age because all I wanted to do was play football. I knew that I was pretty good at football because I was larger than many of my peers. Due to my lack of focus in elementary school, I began to struggle, but did not realize how much I was struggling. In middle school, my father passed away and I began to "act out" in the classroom because I didn't know how to handle his death. At this age, reading was still not on my "to do list" because it seemed tedious. However, I read The Giver by Lois Lowry late in middle school. Although I was hesitant at first because I was not an avid reader, I persevered and read it. This book describes the life of the main character, Jonas. He lives in a society where uniformity and conformity are the norm, and to deviate from this normality is unheard of. The battles that Jonas faces make him a strong character and someone who I could relate to; I was facing some battles myself at this point in my life.

When I entered the ninth grade, my football coach made it clear that I had to start being a better student. I decided that I needed to change and get my head focused. My journey through high school was no smooth coasting. I worked hard on the football field, and pushed myself to my limits every day. But in the classroom I faced grave obstacles. I struggled in English, and in my senior year, I was plagued with passing the English Standard of Learning End of Course test. No matter what I seemed to do to prepare for the test, I still came up short. I had many offers from colleges to play football, but many pulled their offer because I was not yet a certified senior. Yet one university never gave up on me, West Virginia University, and this really encouraged me to keep persevering. It was finally in the summer that I passed the

EOC test and was able to receive my high school diploma. I could have thrown in the towel once colleges gave up on me, but the encouragement of my family, my coaches, and my teachers kept me going. Because those people stuck with me and WVU gave me a chance, I am where I am today: a member of the Tennessee Titans football team.

In hindsight, I realize that if I had kept reading or maybe started valuing reading at a younger age, I may not have experienced the struggle that I did in the classroom. After my freshman year of college, I realized how important reading is to one's success in life. Reading helps with one's critical thinking and analytical skills, which are extremely important skills to have in order to be successful on the football field. I hope my story inspires others, especially athletes, to read every day and to take ownership of the reading.

Quinton Spain attended Petersburg (Va.) High School and is a 2010 graduate. As a young child, Spain and his coaches quickly realized his potential as a football player because of his large size; he now stands at 6 feet 4 inches and 330 pounds. During his high school career at PHS, he played in the U.S. Army All-American game, which is one of the highest honors for a high school football player. As a senior, he scored four touchdowns as a fullback on goal line packages. He collected 103 tackles as a defensive tackle and forced 7 fumbles and recovered 5 fumbles. Also, he recorded 23 tackles for loss, five sacks and had seven games with 10 or more tackles. His outstanding high school career led to his full scholarship to play for West Virginia University.

His time at WVU allowed him to hone his skills as an offensive left guard. Throughout his career, he started numerous games for the Mountaineers, and helped the team to several victories. He started all 13 games during his sophomore, junior, and senior years. In addition, he earned several honors due to his performances such as All-Big 12 Conference third team in his junior year and All-Big 12 first team in his senior year. After his exceptional career at WVU, he entered the

NFL draft in 2015. Although he entered as a free agent, he stood out at the combine he attended and continued to train. In the end, Spain signed with the Tennessee Titans as a rookie free agent; he was one of two to make the 53-man roster. Last season, Spain made his NFL debut against the Raiders and had an incredible game. From this point on, he started for the Titans, helping them improve their statistics on offense.

Reading with Intention

by Fernando Velasco as told to Kathryn Starke

I was born in Wrens, Georgia in a small town with less than 3,000 people. I really liked school growing up. I loved my fourth-grade teacher, who I am still in communication with today. We actually saw our teachers out at the grocery store and around town so school was a big part of my childhood. I have to say, though, I have always been a math guy; I enjoy numbers. I knew that if I wanted to go to college, I had to read and take a liking to it in order for me to cross that bridge. I would read enough to get my assignments done and liked reading about sports, basketball players, or football players.

I saved my money to buy books at the book fair when it came to school. I would usually buy a sports book. My favorite book as a child was Green Eggs and Ham by Dr. Seuss; it was a fun book to read with all of the rhymes. In church, I read scriptures each week. At home, reading was not as strict. I know how important it is to set an example for your children at home, which is why I read nightly to my seventeen-month-old.

When I was five years old, I wanted to be a firefighter. I was intrigued by these heroes saving people's lives. At the age of eight, I started dreaming about being in the NFL. Growing up in Georgia. I loved the Atlanta Falcons but I really didn't have a favorite team growing up. I started watching football on TV and a friend's dad played in the NFL. In fact, he was the last person from our hometown to play in the NFL before me. After high school, I graduated from the University of Georgia before being drafted by the Tennessee Titans.

I definitely use reading in my career as a professional athlete and in everyday life. Today, I would consider myself a great reader. I read books about marriage and family because I didn't see that growing up. Every morning, the first thing I do is read a daily devotional and sports page. It's very important to start reading at a very early age to get that foundation and keep growing as a reader. I founded Right C.H.O.I.C.E.S. Foundation to help youth prepare for their future by understanding their choices and how they impact the future. This year, we celebrated Reading Across America at a local elementary school. We gave away 5,000 books to kids. While reading may not be everyone's favorite activity, we need to encourage all kids to read daily. Anything you want to do in life, you have to be able to read!

Fernando Velasco hails from the University of Georgia where he received a BS in 2008. A Wrens, Georgia native, he is a proud Alum of Jefferson County High School. Fernando entered the NFL in 2008 as an undrafted free agent. After five seasons with the Tennessee Titans, he joined the Pittsburgh Steelers. After a season in Pittsburgh, he joined the Carolina Panthers and was a member of the 2015 Carolina Panthers who made an appearance in Super Bowl 50!! In 2010 Fernando founded Right Choices Foundation with the mission to connect youth participants with opportunities that promote academic excellence and character development! The foundation operates programs in Jefferson County and will launch new programming for the Gwinnett County, Georgia area in 2016. To learn more about RCF you can visit www. rightchoicesfoundation.org

Redskins Read

by Emily King and Allie Pisching

"At a young age, I believe it's important to learn how to read, and learn how to communicate and write. 'Knowledge is power,' and being able to read and write, you can set your goals and dreams."

Coming from a parent, teacher, or friend, this statement doesn't have the same effect on an elementary school student as it does coming from a professional athlete.

But when Colt McCoy, quarterback for the Washington Redskins, made this statement at a Redskins Charitable Foundation event in May 2016, people listened. The seven-year NFL veteran, who graduated from the University of Texas as the winningest quarterback in NCAA history at the time, has a voice magnified by the spotlight of the NFL and his personal successes.

This megaphone of a platform comes with great responsibility.

The impact that professional athletes can have on a child's trajectory is astounding, and the Washington Redskins Charitable Foundation aims to utilize athletes as role models to make a positive and measurable impact on children in the community.

In an effort to make reading more fun for elementary students, the Redskins Charitable Foundation created and launched the Redskins Read Program in 2015, focusing on a playbook for students to study the Xs and Os of reading. The Redskins Read Playbook provides monthly prompts for students to analyze books of their choice, focusing on different areas of the story (e.g., characters, setting, plot). This supplemental learning tool incentivizes fourth- and fifth-grade students by providing monthly prizes and the chance to host a Redskins event with current players at their school. With the ultimate prize of meeting a professional athlete, students are encouraged to work hard in the program individually and as a school to achieve a common goal.

"I am honored and feel privileged to have had this unique opportunity [with the Redskins Read Program]," said one participating teacher. "This, by far, is the greatest accomplishment I have had as a teacher, helping to get students this far in a program with such great purpose."

A positive influence or professional athlete serving as a role model won't directly increase test scores, won't make memorizing vocabulary words any easier, and won't force students to finish homework on time. But an athlete can change an attitude. A positive attitude can make going to school more exciting, make picking up a chapter book a little less scary, and make academic challenges and goals seem attainable.

Washington Redskins safety David Bruton Jr. believes, "As an organization and individually, we owe it to our community to better our youth, and what better way than through literacy. Reading enriches the lives of our youth and gives them a better chance to be successful in life."

For some of the luckier professional athletes, their football home and hometown end up aligning, providing them with the irreplaceable opportunity to give back to the community where they were raised. Washington Redskins offensive lineman Arie Kouandjio grew up minutes from the Redskins' stadium in Prince George's County, Maryland. After a successful college football career — culminating in earning his Master's Degree — at the University of Alabama, Arie found himself back home playing for his hometown team. With a new platform, he was able to visit his elementary school to share the positive messaging about reading through the Redskins Read Program.

"To have one of our own students be so successful and to come back and visit the kids and share the information about how important reading is and showing his success is just a really great boost for our literacy program," said the school principal, who watched Arie grow as a student through elementary school.

Most professional athletes, however, are often thrust into an environment where their only connection to the area is fellow teammates. Oftentimes, connecting with the community is a way to show fans they have embraced their new home as an important next chapter in their lives. Chris Baker, a native of Windsor, Conneticut, is an admirable example of an athlete who recognizes his impact in shaping children's lives, regardless of what city he's in.

"I understand how important reading is for our youth," Chris said. "Reading is fundamental. It's going to help them in every area of their life, whether it's school or whether it's sports. We have to be able to read, so I push them to read as much as possible, especially when you're a youngster. When you get to high school, it's second nature, it's easy. The transition from high school to college is easier if you're able to read and do math and do everything efficiently."

Over the course of 2015, the Redskins Charitable Foundation assisted players like Colt, David, Arie, Chris, and more in sharing their message with students across the D.C. Metro area. In total, 26,842 students were impacted through the Redskins Charitable Foundation's literacy efforts like the Redskins Read Program.

For the more than 25,000 students, the words "practice squad," "starter," or "injured reserve" don't carry the same meaning as they do on the field. In the school and in the classroom, every player is a starter, every player is a role model, and every player has the ability to change the direction of a student's perspective on literacy.

———————

Emily King and Allie Pisching, Community and Charitable Programs, The Washington Redskins

Part 4
Handoffs from Educator to Educator

Reading in 2016

by Matthew T. Maher

I've recently been thinking about what reading means to kids these days. What I've discovered is that it means something different to each of them. Some absolutely love it and lose themselves in it. It is their most favorite thing. However, it probably will not shock you to find out that not all of your young people feel that way. We all know that many kids are drawn to the more shiny visual mediums, where the imaginative work is done for them. It's hard to blame them really. You've seen these gigantic screens in high definition. You've probably played or watched someone else playing these incredible interactive video games. I have to admit, it's quite alluring. So where does reading fit in? Why would a child chose a plain old book over these bright and shiny things?

Well, I suppose it starts early in life. Read to your babies, keep reading to them as they grow up, give them access to books, take them to the library, and let them see you read. That should do it, right? As a father of two teenagers, I can tell you this is not a sure fire plan! My wife and I did all of these things, and we have two reluctant readers. Where did we go wrong? Was it because we let them watch TV? Use a computer? Get cellphones (at age 13)? I don't know. They are both capable readers, they just don't love it the way we did at their age, maybe that's okay. We all develop different likes as we get older, maybe reading is one of things, like golf or gardening that you develop an interest in later. If we can at least arm them with that skill they will have the opportunity to make that choice for themselves down the road.

Maybe it's not the end of the world if a child doesn't love to read, maybe it doesn't make us a bad parent or an ineffective teacher; they don't have to love everything. It is, however, vitally important that they know how to read and that they understand the importance of being a skilled reader. They need to know that, more than anything else, it is the academic ability that they will use most; in fact, they will use it every day. It is our job to make sure every child has the opportunity to become a proficient reader, whether they like it or not!

Being a public school principal, facing this reading dilemma, I took it upon myself to try to do something. What if we created an environment that promoted reading, not only for knowledge acquisition but also to help students create, think, and imagine? What would this look like? What would it mean to student learning? In 2014 we created three classrooms that centered on students and what they are interested in, we gave them more technology, we had them work together in groups, we allowed them to create, not just absorb, and made reading a central part of all of it. This year we have seven of these Design for Excellence classes, and the results continue to make us smile. What we are learning is that out students will read, and might even enjoy reading if we make it relevant and interesting to them. Our charge is to adapt our teaching to this generation, we have to figure out what makes them tick and then challenge them to do something with it!

As someone who has chosen to read this book, you know how important reading is; you will do your best to instill the love of reading in every child you reach. Sometimes it will work, sometimes though you will feel defeated by those competing forces that steal our children's attention. Don't beat yourself up, don't give up, keep fighting the good fight, and know that not all victories are immediately realized.

Matt Maher, *parent, principal, educator*

A Small Investment

by Siri Roma

When I was sixteen, the thing I wanted most wasn't a car. It wasn't clothes. It wasn't even a boyfriend. Nope. It was a full set of Pleasant Company dolls with all of the accompanying clothes, furniture, and accessories. Oh, and of course...the books. I'd been a fan since I was eight. Now some of you may be judging me. (Isn't sixteen a little old to be playing with dolls?) Some of you will be making excuses for me. (Well, she did have a younger sister. Maybe that kept her socially behind her peers?) Others have already stopped reading this, convinced I'm sheer cray cray. But the rest of you recognize a bit of yourself in this confession and know what I'm talking about. How easy it is to become so immersed in the world of a book that you do everything you can to stay in that world even after you tear your eyes from the page or, god forbid, finish it. How you find yourself, as you go about your day-to-day life, wondering about the characters in that parallel universe you step into each time you crack open the binding. What are they up to now while you're away? What are you missing? And how soon can you get back? I've had that experience with books several times, but it was the relatable history stories in what later became the American Girls book series that first filled me with that kind of obsessive rapture.

Cue my mother, the woman ultimately responsible for my love of these books (having provided them to me) and a big proponent of education. With four children in the public school system, she developed a good rapport with our teachers whom she saw again and again every couple of years as we passed through the grades. She volunteered for years, mentoring kids who needed extra one-on-one tutoring in various subjects. She threw her all into those kids, including buying one of them a guitar when he expressed an interest.

At one point, she knew the teachers at our school system were attempting to expand the reading program at the middle school. My mom asked what she could do to help, and offered up an idea for an after-school reading club featuring the books I'd enjoyed so much – an American Girls book club. She'd be the moderator, the attendees would be required to buy one book of their own and do some solo reading in between meetings, and they'd all meet once a week. The teachers thought it was a fabulous idea and gave her some names of sixth-grade girls who could benefit from some extra reading support. My mom sent notes to the students' parents for permission and all was a go. First and foremost my mom wanted the club to be a fun activity that the girls looked forward to and not a prison sentence they would grudgingly endure. So she made time for socializing at the beginning of the meeting, as sixth-grade girls have a lot to say and would have a good time getting to know one another. And she brought in a themed snack depending on what they were reading for the day: Samantha's jelly biscuits, Felicity's spiced nuts, Addy's sweet potato pie, Molly's carrot sticks (World War II rationing was not for the faint of heart). Finally, every time the girls came to session, they got a raffle ticket for a chance to win an American Girl doll.

During the meetings, they'd read aloud a chapter or couple of chapters, round robin style, and discuss the books. When the girls in the club compared stories about their lives and those of the historical characters they were reading about, they noticed lots of differences ("Girls used to wear a lot more underwear back then, didn't they?") but also many similarities. One girl stuck out in my mom's mind. Let's call her Laura. Laura was one of the eldest children in a very large, poor family. She helped raise her younger siblings and worked on the family farm. My mom didn't imagine she had many pleasures in her life, but she seemed to really take to one of the characters in the book series: Kirsten Larsen, a Swedish immigrant farm girl in the 1850s. Laura could relate to getting up early to tend to livestock as well as feeling timid in school. You can imagine how pleased my mother was when Laura was the recipient of the final doll prize! A shy girl, Laura gained not only a better handle on reading as a result of the book club but also a new circle of friends and a confidence to tackle challenges that lay ahead in middle school and beyond.

My mom wasn't anything special on the outside. She had no unique pedagogical skills to bring to the table other than a desire to do something to help out. You know one of the best parts of this story? She was a busy lady, a nurse, a working mother of four, but she made time for what she believed in. She considered taking a couple hours out of her week to mentor these girls a small investment of her time for a big payoff in these girls' education. She went on to become a member of our school board, continuing to champion literacy.

I'd love to say all those girls grew up to be super readers, English or history professors or editors, as it'd make a perfect Hallmark ending to this story. Truthfully, I have no idea where they are now. What I hope for them, however, is now that they're all grown up, maybe with kids of their own or maybe not, that they think back to that time when my mom came into their lives and put together this book club. Maybe the sight of their old American girl books will spark a memory, and they'll remember their sixth-grade year when an unknown lady took an interest in them. Maybe they'll be inspired to pass it forward, to volunteer at a school themselves, to mentor a struggling student, to be good citizens who realize it takes a village to raise an educated community. What if we all were?

Siri Roma, Librarian

Tackle Summer Reading

by Donna McIndoe Dalton

I remember the smell of visiting my first public library. Seriously. The smell. Perhaps it was the paper from the pages in each book. Or possibly it was the glue from the binding that held the pages together. Maybe it was the ink that brought the stories in the books to life. Even today, I get a sniff of "scent-amental" nostalgia whenever I walk into a library.

Now that I reflect about it, perhaps it was the fragrance of knowledge that I experienced in that small library on Belmont Avenue. Or the scent of adventure. Or the perfume of learning. Whatever we want to call it, I caught my first enticing whiff of summer reading and the love of books that day.

My visit to the library was anything but inevitable.

My family did not have money for vacation trips or summer camps. There were no libraries within walking distance. My dad drove our only car to work each day, so my mom had no way to drive us to the public library. And to top it off, school libraries were closed tight — after all, it was summer and learning was over for the next three months.

Luckily, my friend's mom did have a car, and I very well remember the first day she loaded a bunch of neighborhood kids up and drove us to the local public library.

My love of summer reading started that day.

My friend's mom signed me up for a library card and drove us back and forth to the library throughout the summer. Now I could check out books that piqued my interest, bring them home and devour them curled up on our side porch or under the shade of a backyard tree.

Ahhh, the joys of summer reading: No book reports due and no shadow boxes (now we call them dioramas) required. Just the freeness of reading for pleasure, for fun, for adventure, for escape. That was more than 50 years ago.

Fast forward to today, when I serve as the chief academic officer in Chesterfield County Public Schools, located next to Richmond, Virginia. Many of our families are in the same situation as my family was 50 years ago: They have limited access to books and other educational opportunities during the summer.

Our school division with more than 58,000 students and 63 schools includes 17 Title 1 schools. Almost 40% of our students qualify for free or reduced-price meals. Some of our students lose academic knowledge over the summer. Parents work. Students have no way to get to public libraries during the day. Disadvantaged students often fall behind academically. It's sometimes referred to as the "summer slide."

Here's one difference between my childhood and today: Educators now realize that learning cannot take a three-month vacation, especially for students from less-well-to-do families.

As a school district, we purposely paused to think through how we could reverse the summer reading slide. Chesterfield County Public Schools decided to tackle the issue in multiple ways. As part of our strategic innovation plan, the Design for Excellence 2020, Chesterfield County Public Schools created a comprehensive K-12 summer reading plan beginning in 2013. We incorporated into our approach research conducted by Anne McGill-Franzen and Richard Allington (2004) that suggests when a child reads as few as six appropriately leveled books, he or she is likely to fend off summer reading loss and maintain reading gains made during the previous school year.

Clearly, we needed to get books into the hands of our children for the summer and we needed to motivate students to read those books.

Under the leadership of our superintendent, Dr. Marcus Newsome, Chesterfield County Public Schools forged a partnership with the county library system and the Washington Redskins Charitable Foundation to create Redskins Read for the summer of 2014.

We kicked off Redskins Read during an event in the public libraries—CCPS Night at the Public Libraries. The public libraries stayed open late to welcome our families, provide recommended reading lists, register students for library cards, and show how to participate in Redskins Read by logging minutes.

In the Redskins Read program, every 10 minutes a student read equaled a yard and 100 minutes equaled a touchdown. Students who scored the most touchdowns won prizes, classes won visits with writers, and the top elementary school won a reading pep rally with Redskins players. To motivate students, Washington Redskins players recorded messages that families received via phone calls throughout the summer.

Summer reading + an exciting pro football connection = a winning combination for students! Our students read and logged more than 6 million minutes in the summer of 2014. One middle school student, Joy, read more than 2,900 minutes. When asked how she did it, she said she read after lunch, at bedtime, and even during car rides.

In the summer of 2015, we added a second summer reading partnership that included local business, community, and faith partners. Initiated by two dynamic members of the Chesterfield County School Board, Carrie Coyner and Dianne Smith, the Summer Star Reading Program was born! Focusing on high-poverty schools and selecting a community within that school boundary, community partners created Little Free Libraries for targeted communities. Plans for building the little libraries were made available via Pinterest and littlefreelibrary.org. Though there was no size requirement, we wanted the little libraries to be large enough to offer a variety of books for elementary, middle, and high school students as well as their parents. Little libraries popped up in apartment complexes, community centers, in front of houses, at pools, and even at schools. Each little library community team maintained and restocked the libraries. Local churches helped collect books for the little libraries, including books written in Spanish for neighborhoods with large Latino populations. Events were hosted in the community, at pools, at community centers, and at churches to draw students to the little libraries. Crafts were made. Snacks were provided. And children got to choose books to take home and read.

In addition, at twenty-six high-poverty schools, twenty at-risk students were identified to receive five books through the mail over the summer. The students picked out the books, thinking they were choosing books for their classmates. Books were mailed throughout the summer to students with personal notes from principals tucked inside. Imagine the delight of students who unexpectedly received books to keep forever.

For the summer of 2016, Chesterfield remains committed to reversing the summer slide, investing to help each school develop a personalized summer reading plan for their students. Vans driven by principals will move out into the community stocked with books, competitions will be held, school libraries will stay open, and events are planned to draw the community into the schools.

Through our summer reading initiatives, we are not just helping students academically — we are also creating treasured memories connected to summer reading. You better believe our students will remember fifty years from now the fun of taking a book from a Little Free Library or how great it was to see their principal driving a bookmobile or the joy of finding a book in their mailbox. Our hope is that our students will become lifelong readers and lifelong learners.

What are your favorite memories of summer reading? And how can you use your memories — even your scent memory — to help a community read? Let's bring the fun of summer reading back to life for our students: Let's tackle the summer reading slide!

Donna McIndoe Dalton is the Chief Academic Officer for Chesterfield County Public Schools.

Learning to Read Through Tennis

by Becky Holmes

Tennis and reading, yes—those two words can go together in the same sentence. As a mom of three elementary-age kids, former kindergarten teacher, author of a children's tennis book, and tennis coach…I find myself putting those two words together quite frequently. We all know kids like to have fun and be active, so what better way to learn than through active play?! Whether you are playing tennis, baseball, gymnastics, football, basketball, dance, or soccer, any coach or parent should be "teaching" as well as coaching.

Here is a sample lesson plan on how I incorporate learning to read through my tennis classes:

Sample Toddlers & Tennis lesson plan:

Who ~ 8 children in the class, age 5

Length of class ~ 45 minutes

Theme ~ Introduction to tennis

List equipment needed

Warm up ~

Exercise dice: using 2 colorful dice, one with different exercises and one with numbers, each child in the class will get the chance to throw the soft, large dice to see what exercise all the kids will do. Example: 6 jumping jacks

For the coach: How can you incorporate reading here? Ask the kids to look at the first letter of the word "jumping" jacks, and what sound does a letter "J" make?" Let's sound out the word together (jumping). Then, asked the kids what number the dice landed on. Next, the kids perform the exercise.

Activities ~

Coach has laid out different colors shapes with sticker letters on each. Example: blue circle with letter "A"
      Coach Says: Max, will you please go stand on the shape with the letter that makes the "A" sound? Max will go stand on the blue circle with the letter "A" on it. Coach will ask what letter it is, a word that begins with the letter, and the shape and color he is standing on. Max: I am standing on a blue circle with the letter "A" like an apple. Coach helps as needed.

Continue on with tennis activities...

Game ~

Parachute: using a parachute with the primary colors on it each child will choose a color to hold. Coach asks students the color they chose and working together to sound out the words and spell it aloud. Example: green
I like to wrap up several of my classes by reading a book to the kids. It is either tennis related, using good character traits, and/or staying healthy. I love it when it involves all of the above.

Tips to reading to a group of kids:

*Make sure everyone can see the book and pictures.

*Ask questions to keep the kids engaged.

*What is the cover page? How do you think this character is feeling? What do you think is going to happen next? These are all good questions to ask when reading a book to kids.

*Talk about what the job of the author and the illustrator is.

*Praise the kids for being good listeners.

Kids get a colorful happy hand stamp or sticker at the end of tennis class.

Happy playing and happy reading!

Becky Holmes ~ *Founder/Owner of Toddlers & Tennis,*
Author of Totally Tennis For Me
Facebook: Toddlers and Tennis/Totally Tennis For Me
Instagram: beckstennis
www.toddlersandtennis.com

Brilliant Book Talks

by Laura Barrick

My love for reading and books began at a very young age. I always had a book in hand. I would read in the car, while running errands with my mother. I would read during television commercials. I fortunately took to it naturally, and that passion for reading is still with me today as a young adult. While I love to delve into a new story, what I love even more is to share a story with a friend and have a great conversation about it. I love sharing the excitement and emotion that I feel when I read a book, with someone else who has a shared experience. It is like leaving a theater and talking with everyone about the best parts of the show. I think back on my early education, and I consider where this passion for sharing a good story started.

Then, I remember how much I enjoyed the school assignment of "book reports." While many students probably met these projects with dread, I never failed to brainstorm a creative idea and excitedly share it with my class. Just last month, my mother sent me a box of my childhood artwork and projects. The memories flooded back. I found an old metal hanger, fashioned into a mobile, with the characters of Matilda hanging by threadbare tape. I discovered a movie poster I had designed, featuring the book I just read as the newest mystery movie. I can recall standing before my class and pitching to my peers to go see Who Stole the Wizard of Oz? Then I remember the video-taped book report I recorded. I dressed up as a train conductor and stood on my parent's fireplace shouting, "All aboard the Boxcar children! All Aboard!" My sister sat in the background and blew a train whistle, while my parents filmed me talking about one of my favorite childhood series, The Boxcar Children.

I met each of these assignments with such passion and

animation – surely my teachers found it amusing while classmates cringed at the idea of presenting in front of their peers. However, I was motivated by desire to share a great story. Book reports and creative assignments from my youth instilled a passion for reading, but importantly a desire to share that passion for reading. To this day, my friends and family reach out for a good book recommendation as they are heading off on vacation. They know I am eager to share, and that I will be even more eager to find out how that story made them feel.

Laura Barrick, *avid reader*

A New Angle to Create Equity in Education

by Dr. Joshua P. Cole

As an elementary school principal, I believe the first step to address reading is to name our diversity. In order to empower students, families, and communities with the skills of literacy, we as educators must know who we are supporting and what is needed in order to support our students as thriving readers. This process begins with relationships that require an ongoing conversation about how to truly meet the needs of all students in order to increase literacy skills, which will ultimately create equity in education. In order to be successful with this goal, a culture of open-mindedness is particularly important within a school setting between staff members, families, community partners, and especially the students. Everyone truly believing in the potential of their students creates opportunities for success. In my role as a principal, I have found that this goal must be focused on the love of literacy. It is significantly essential to facilitate conversations about out-of-the box ideas to help meet the literacy needs of all students.

One out-of-the box idea I have implemented is focusing on empowering students with social emotional learning through the "super powers" of The Character Club. Focusing on character traits that have morphed into The Character Club of everyday super heroes empowers students with invaluable skills to be successful in school and in life. Gratitude: Appreciation for others and opportunities for success. Curiosity: Eagerness to explore new things. Social Intelligence: Respecting the feelings of others to solve conflicts. Self-Control: Responsible actions with school work and interpersonal skills. Optimism: Belief in overcoming frustrations to improve self. Grit: Perseverance and focus on finishing tasks. Zest: Active participation and enthusiasm for life

and learning.

The Character Club also includes a robot computer, Query, who computes written requests of needs from students and shares these needs with The Character Club superheroes, who in turn write back to the students with an empowering message of positive support. This process encourages students to become excited about literacy through their own writing to Query and their reading of ideas from The Character Club to be "super heroes" themselves!

Children need to see, hear, and feel that it is acceptable to write about their needs as well as to ask for support so they can improve themselves for the betterment of their futures. Through the vehicle of education, focused on the love of literacy, is how I believe we can break the cycle of inequities in education for future generations to live in a more harmonious world.

To learn more about my focus on creating equity in education, please visit: www.joshuapcole.com.

Joshua P. Cole, Ph.D.
Milken Educator
Principal

Growing Up in Kindergarten

by Mary Burns Ackerly

My first year of teaching was in a Title 1 school. It was a busy and stressful first year as I worked with my new kindergarten class. They were full of energy and loved coming to school. They were experiencing so many things for the first time, but there is one thing that I learned that first year from them that has strengthened by love for teaching kindergarten to children in need – the amazing things that happen in a garden, regardless of the size, with the young mind and heart of a kindergartner.

I grew up with a garden in my backyard when I was little. There were always tomatoes, all different kinds of tomatoes. My dad loved tomatoes. I did not care for them when I was young, but I loved watching them grow and picking them when they were ready. There is something about working with your hands, being hands-on, that is perfect for a young mind.

Kindergarten is the year children build their foundation in learning to prepare them for years to come as they go through school. Toward the end of that school year, kindergarteners start learning about life cycles. The curriculum had seeds for my class to plant in clear plastic cups to watch grow. We did it. Their eyes opened. We placed the clear cups on a table by the window where the seeds would get sun to help them grow. The class would go look whenever they had a chance to see if anything had changed. When the roots appeared, their eyes opened bigger. When the stem popped out, their eyes were even bigger.

I realized that this was something they had never seen before. We had talked about plants, the life cycle, and where you find them. They listened, but it was not until they saw the roots and the stem that they understood. Vegetables and fruits did not just appear at Walmart, they grew on a farm from a tiny seed. My class was mesmerized. A new door opened.

As we watched our new seedlings grow, we made a class list of our favorite vegetables. We picked two and the next day I arrived with two pots, soil and two seedlings – tomato and pepper. That afternoon we sat outside our backdoor and planted our two seedlings. Everyone had a chance to put a cupful of soil in the pots and help plant our new seedlings. Their eyes were sparkling. The pots sat right outside the backdoor; we watered them every day and watched them grow.

The tomatoes and the peppers were "the talk" of the class. We talked about them. We wrote about them. We drew pictures of them. We read books about them. I read as many books as I could get my hands about plants and the plant life cycle. We did math activities with tomatoes and peppers. We made the life cycle of a tomato. We did everything.

Then they arrived at school one morning and looked out the window like they always did to see if there were any changes. There was jumping and shouting! There was lots of it! The tomatoes had started to turn red and the peppers were bigger. This was the first time my class had ever seen tomatoes change color. Remember, before we planted our tomato and pepper plant, they thought tomatoes and peppers just came from Walmart. Now they had seen the plants grow and change. They wanted to see more.

Once our class tomatoes and peppers were finally ready to be picked, we sat outside and cut them up. They got to see the tiny seeds that could one day grow up to be a tomato plant or a pepper plant. They each got a slice of the two vegetables on a napkin. Some of them had never had a fresh tomato or pepper. I suggested that they all try, because you never know if you will like it unless you try! I started the count of three which had become a regular routine in the classroom to quiet down, to have a seat, to get in line, to eat snack. They knew when I said three, they could eat. One…two…three!!

That was the beginning. The fact that the kindergarten mind falls in love with the garden is one of the amazing things I have learned teaching kindergarten. My two pots went to six pots with more vegetables and the addition of herbs. They even got to sprout their own vegetable to take home and grow. But I have been incredibly lucky. I met Backyard Farmers and Fit4Kids. They helped me start a garden at my school. The students helped build it and learned to take care of it, their garden. Now we have a learning garden. It has made an incredible impact on my class, the students at my school, the faculty, and the parents. We use it year round. The students learn to plant, maintain, pick, and cook the vegetables and herbs they grow. It has made an impact on every child, every age.

The garden teaches them about plants, working together, healthy habits and choices, and so much more. The garden starts with just one seed. Start growing!

A collection of a few of my favorites that my classes have loved…

The Tiny Seed by Eric Carle

Flower Garden by Eve Bunting

The Ugly Vegetables by Grace Lin

A Fruit is a Suitcase for Seeds by Jean Richards

Up in the Garden and Down in the Dirt

Plant Secrets by Emily Goodman

by Kate Messner

Little Pea by Amy Krouse Rosenthal

Vegetable Garden by Douglas Florian

Changes by Marjorie N. Allen and Shelley Rotner

If You Hold a Seed by Elly MacKay

Math Around Us: Sorting at the Market

Growing a Garden by Mari Schuh

by Tracey Steffora

Calendar by Myra Gohn Livingston

Sunflower House by Eve Bunting

Seeds and Weeds by Rena K. Kirkpatrick

City Green by DyAnne DiSalvo-Ryan
Tops & Bottoms Adapted by Janet Stevens
How a Seed Grows by Helens J. Jordan
How Do Plants Get Food? By Meish Goldish
Eat Your Peas, Louise! By Pegeen Snow
Bread is for Eating by David & Phillis Gershator
Plants by Terry Jennings
Growing Vegetable Soup by Lois Ehlert
Planting a Rainbow by Lois Ehlert
It's Our Garden by George Ancona
Spring is Here, A Story About Seeds
Animals in the Garden by Melvin & Gilda
By John Holub Berger
Bugs in the Garden by Catherine Hapka
My Five Senses by Margaret Miller
Splat the Cat, Oopsie-Daisy by Rob Scotton

Fit4Kids www.grfit4kids.org
Agriculture in the Classroom www.agintheclass.org

———————

Mary Burns Ackerly *graduated from the University of Virginia with a BA in Sociology and received her Master in Teaching from Mary Baldwin College. She has been teaching kindergarten for 11 years. She spent one year teaching in Honduras at the Alison Bixby Stone School and has taught in the Richmond area for ten years. Teaching in the school learning garden is her personal passion.*

The Gift of Reading

by Elizabeth Starke

I understand ideas of giftedness as an actual gift or present. One opens birthday or Christmas gifts each year. Most of the time, the child sees this box wrapped in beautiful colors and paper wondering what lies in store on opening that gift. A child may watch the box, shake it, and explore the shape using the five senses. When the exciting day finally comes, a child opens the box and can experience an array of emotions such as excitement, anger, wonder, or disappointment. If the gift comes with directions or parents explain how to use the gift, then the child can become knowledgeable on how to use the gift. However, if the gift just sits and the child does not explore how to use it on its own, then the child does not understand all the possibilities that could have happened with this gift. In the same way a child who is gifted can be unsure about what special traits and skills the child might possess. The child will explore on its own, yet a strong support system of parents and teachers makes a difference in the success. Also, if the child is not encouraged to practice various skills and gifts, then the child cannot develop the talent further.

Teachers and parents play a crucial role in the literacy development of young gifted children. They need to identify a student's gifts in reading and provide opportunities to utilize gifts through reading a variety of materials. Gifted students may have advanced reading skills, strong vocabulary, and creative writing skills. These traits allow a child to develop advanced skills in a nurturing, stimulating environment. Oftentimes gifted readers can read one to two reading levels above their peers and have a mature level of comprehension of themes presented in books. Teachers and parents needs to assist children to find appropriate leveled books and allow them to explore various themes presented in books.

Gifted readers possess advanced critical thinking skills to analyze different components of a text and they possess a strong sense of empathy where they can relate to characters. Lessons and activities need to promote these higher level thinking skills to encourage the gifted reader. The imagination and inquisitive nature of gifted children allows them to hypothesize aspects of stories and desire to research and learn more about topics presented in the reading material. These children need an opportunity to create projects based on their interest sparked from reading.

One can view giftedness as having a special given gift to think, create, or express one's self in superior ways in comparison to one's peer group. One who is gifted sees aspects of the world in a different way and has the potential to expand the gift for the future. Supportive parents and teachers must nurture this gift by embracing the unique characteristics of gifted readers and allowing their gift to shine and spread light to others.

Elizabeth Starke, Assistant Head of School, St. Nicholas School, Chattanooga, Tennessee.

Never Too Late: 70-Year-Old First Grader

by Alesia Hamilton

Alferd's Story...

Alferd Williams was born in Eudora, Arkansas, December 22, 1937. He was the fourth of nine children. He was eight when he went to work in the fields helping his sharecropper father.

His mother could read some, his father not at all. Alferd's twin brother Jesse would sneak off to school each morning, while Alferd would stay home to help his parents in the fields. His mother would cry when he didn't go to school, but knew that someone had to stay home to help. Alferd said his mom prayed that "someday" he would be able to go to school and learn to read. That never happened for Alferd as a child.

Alferd struggled to work as a young adult. Jobs that did not require reading were hard to come by. Somehow he was able to become employed as a metal worker and a roofer. By 1998, he found himself in a homeless shelter in St. Louis. He contacted his brother, Albert, ten years his senior, who helped him get to St. Joseph, Missouri, where Alferd's "someday" finally came.

Mrs. Hamilton

I was raised, one of six siblings, on a farm outside of Hannibal, Missouri. I attended Southwest Baptist University and graduated from Hannibal LaGrange College with a BSE. Later, I earned my MSE from Baker University. I began my teaching career in Hannibal, and taught second grade, kindergarten, then Reading Recovery for seven years.

I taught first grade at Fairfield, Texas, and Waco, Texas. I moved to St. Joseph in 1998 and began teaching there.

I currently teach first grade at Humboldt Elementary.

My husband Lonnie, our English bulldogs Willie and Betty, and I all live happily ever after in Savannah, Missouri.

Alferd and Mrs. Hamilton....

Alferd Williams was a 68-year-old caretaker for some Edison Elementary children. I first assumed that Alferd was the grandfather, but later discovered that he was a family friend that cared for the three children and got them to/from school daily. In the fall of 2005, Alferd brought a child to my first grade classroom. One day after school I asked Alferd about a note I had sent home with the child. He informed me that he was unable to read. I suggested several community resources; but he declined help saying he had tried in the past, and people just didn't have the patience to teach him. Alferd continued to be in our midst every school day, bringing and picking up those three children. He greeted everyone with his smile that lit up the hallway. There was something special about that man.

Toward the end of the school year, in the spring of 2006, Alferd approached me to say he was ready to learn to read. Once again, I started to tell him of resources, but he quickly stopped me to say, "No, I want YOU to teach me to read." He told me that day that he saw in me the patience and persistence to teach him. His goal was to be able to read the Bible for himself. I had never taught anyone over eight years old to read, but after consulting with family and friends I took up this challenge.

That summer, Alferd and I spent countless hours in the school library. He would arrive at Summer School dismissal time every day. We stayed late into the afternoons. He continued on in July, then in August. No one was watching as Alferd grew as a reader, and I grew as a person—watching his life change before my eyes.

He consumed every bit of literacy I had to offer him! He was finally learning to read! He couldn't get enough of books; I couldn't get enough of his devotion and passion for learning! That summer a bond was created. First we were Learner and Teacher, soon we became Friend and Friend.

In the fall, I invited Alferd to become a volunteer in our classroom. I KNEW Alferd would soak up all that literacy that he had missed as a child. I never expected him to attend first grade every day, but he did. I never expected Alferd to become a major part of our lives, but he did. Every day Alferd began his day with us at 8:00 a.m. and he stayed until lunchtime. He had become one of us. He read when we read. He wrote when we wrote. He LAUGHED when we laughed. We became this magical community of learners, 7 to 70. No one would have believed the connection as both generations learned together, blind to the differences between them and their best friend Alferd.

By November, 2006, Oprah had heard of Alferd's endeavors and invited us to visit her show. Since that time we were fortunate to also visit Ellen Degeneres and have a conversation with Bill Cosby – his favorite author. After being featured in the April, 2008, issue of *People Magazine*, we were chosen one of four *People Magazine*'s Heroes of the Year and were a part of the CNN Tribute to Heroes featured on CNN on Thanksgiving, 2008. Letters telling of Alferd's inspiration poured in from all over the United States. Children and adults had been touched by his dedication to read and realization that it's never too late to learn.

For eight years Alferd attended our first grade classroom every day. Alferd's life completely changed. He became independent and didn't have to rely on anyone else to read for him. His Children's Bible was in his satchel that he carried to and from school, along with his favorite Lil' Bill book. Alferd's goal was to become a strong enough reader that he may someday attend college.

Alferd was an angel that fell down upon our school. He used to say he didn't know what he'd do without us, but truly, we didn't know what we'd ever do without him. He is our HERO that showed friends how important it was to learn to read. What a role model for us all—young and old alike!

The man who once wandered the aisles of the grocery store,

didn't know the difference between junk mail and bills, and couldn't write his own name became a GENIUS (in his own words!) right in front of our eyes. At 70, Alferd proclaimed that anyone could learn to read if they just wanted to. Well, I guess my friend Alferd just wanted to!

In March, 2015, at the young age of 77, our precious friend Alferd passed away. A hero to all who knew him, he changed lives.

Alferd lives on in the hearts of those first grade friends who learned and loved right alongside him. Alferd lives on in the walls of every school he entered. Alferd lives in on the soul of one teacher who learned that it's NEVER TOO LATE for your dreams.

Thank you Alferd.

Alesia Hamilton lives in Savannah, Missouri, with her husband Lonnie and two English bulldogs Willie and Betty. She is a first-grade teacher in the St. Joseph School District in St. Joseph, Missouri, and has taught for 27 years. She and Alfred shared some memorable moments speaking to students, educators, and others, encouraging them to reach for their dreams while conveying Alferd's message - it's NEVER TOO LATE.

Inspiration That Makes A Difference

by Arlise S. Carson

As a young child, I grew up in a low-income community of Portsmouth, Virginia, which is part of the Hampton Roads metropolitan area. While in kindergarten, my mother and father went through a divorce while he was serving time in prison. As a single parent of three young children, she worked multiple jobs to provide for our basic needs. While successfully keeping a roof over our heads and food on our table, she also saturated our home with so much love.

Her commitment to our overall success was filled with a determination that was second to none. Her attitude toward education overshadowed the monthly food stamps and the stigma that comes with being on welfare and living in low-income housing. With her guidance, I quickly realized that our financial state could not diminish our collective and individual value and our small home couldn't hold hostage our enormous dreams.

Even with my mother's encouraging words ringing in my ears, I still experienced a personal struggle when I tried and dared to believe that I was smart enough, mattered to someone, and could accomplish something great. I remember being in school, feeling frightened and all alone as I sat at my desk looking at pages covered with so many new words. The thought of reading for enjoyment and understanding was overwhelming. My eyes filled with tears as I struggled to comprehend what was being read to me. I was lost in my learning and would do all I could to keep the tears from rolling down my cheeks and then it happened, the merging of two great entities.

Suddenly, the words that rang so proud and true from my mother's mouth were caught up in a whirlwind powered by the determination of a third-grade teacher who believed not only in me but also in all of her students. This teacher's faith in me fueled my self-esteem to not only believe I could become a better reader but also a student who could make the impossible possible.

My third-grade teacher's influence on my life became the catalyst for me pursuing a career in education. While sitting in her class, the words on the pages no longer intimidated me because my struggles were embraced by her ability to teach me how to become a great reader. While building my confidence, she reminded me that I am smart and somebody wonderful and I can do anything. This unknown hero may not wear a cape, nor fly in the sky, but she taught me how to soar in my reading. I am forever grateful for this educator who dared to believe in me.

The combination of my mother's words and this teacher's efforts produced in me a love for learning that has carried on for over three decades. Since they took the time to lovingly teach me, I became the first person in my family to graduate from college and earn several master degrees. Their teachings equipped me with the skills needed to become a better reader who could visit new and exciting places just by the turning of a page. Now, I am able to do this honorable and distinctive task for so many other children that are now walking in the shoes that I once walked in myself.

To every student in America, I say to you, "You are great and you can read!" Don't give up, believe in yourself, and know that you can do the impossible!

To every parent in America, I say to you, "You are our first role model; nurture us, shape us and help us believe we can be great."

To every teacher, I say to you, "Teach us, inspire us and please don't leave us behind."

———————

Arlise Carson, Principal, Hempstead Schools, New York

Teaching Tools with a Twist

by Libby Daniels and Spencer Cross

Title 1 teacher Spencer Cross and Regular Ed second-grade teacher Libby Daniels team taught reading for a year. We are going to share a unit that the students seemed to enjoy the most. It was a lesson on community helpers and the tools the community helpers needed to perform the job. It incorporated nonfiction and fictional texts, a Social Studies lesson, a writing activity, as well as oral dramatic activities to enhance reading fluency and other text structures to increase comprehension.

Day 1
We introduced the vocabulary from the texts *TOOLS THAT HELP* and *HELPING OUT.*

+We played a game of Matching the Vocabulary Word with a kid-friendly definition.

+We played a game of Fill in the Blank using the vocabulary words.

+We played a game of <u>Slap</u> by writing the vocabulary words on the board and the students used a fly swatter to slap the correct word based on the definition.

Day 2
Our focus today was on Reader's Theater.
First, the students and teachers read the text *TOOLS THAT HELP* by Beverly A.Dietz in a guided reading setting. Then, the students read the same text with a partner.

Next, the students chose one of the jobs from the text that they would read aloud to the class. They practiced reading their part, and then they dressed in the appropriate clothes for the job as well as chose the tools they would need to perform the job. Then, the students read their part aloud to the class and their peers critiqued them on their performance based on fluency, expression and enthusiasm. Finally, the students chose a partner to interview about his/her job. The teachers provided the students with the questions to ask as well as a play microphone to use like a reporter. The partners took turns being the reporter and writing the answers to each other's questions during the interview. As an exit ticket, different students shared their partners' interviews aloud with their classmates

The teacher took a picture of each student dressed for the job to be used for a display in the classroom.

Day 3

Today's focus was on the Main Idea of the story *HELPING OUT.* The students reviewed the vocabulary discussed on Day 1. The students then read the story *HELPING OUT* in a guided reading setting.

We played a game of Facts OR Fibs to discuss the main idea of the story.

The teachers wrote the main idea of each page of the story on strips of paper along with some details that may or may not belong with that specific main idea. The strips were put in envelopes marked with the page number. Each student chose an envelope and the students had to choose if the strips inside the envelopes were a fact or a fib based on that page in the story they read.

Day 4

Today's focus was on Comprehension Questions to review the story *HELPING OUT* to help prepare for the assessment on Friday. The students read the story *HELPING OUT* with a partner. The students then played a game of Pass the Envelope Please. The teachers wrote comprehension questions on strips of paper. The students took turns choosing a strip from the envelope and picking a classmate to answer the question. Continue this activity until all students have had a chance to answer a question.

Day 5
Today was assessment day. We created one that focused on the comprehension skills and vocabulary that went with our unit text.

Spencer Cross is a Title I teacher and Libby Daniels is a second-grade regular education teacher in Lynchburg City Public Schools in Lynchburg, Virginia.

"Fostering" a Love of Reading

by Lindsey Kistner

I am a foster mom. I have seen babies and toddlers form attachments that they so desperately need and desire. I have even been privileged enough to remain in contact with one of the newborns that was in our care, and I can see the positive effects that attachment provided her in the short time she was with us. I have seen older children learn to trust my husband and me to the point where they feel comfortable enough to start talking about their personal experiences and feelings, and they begin to see themselves as special and worthy citizens in society. This leads them to begin healing from their past and to start planning for their future. There are many ways that these types of relationships form, but reading together is one of my favorites. Reading provides special, uninterrupted time with children. It provides topics for conversation, laughs, tears, and wonderment. It provides the opportunity to bond and build trust with children through shared experiences.

My family and I take in children of all ages with all sorts of backgrounds. Because these children have been removed from their environment for things such as neglect and/or abuse, they are in desperate need of love, attachment, confidence, and more. The experience of reading to, and with, these children has shown me, firsthand, some of the benefits of reading that I seemed to take advantage of with my own children before we became a foster family. I'm here to tell you that there is a long list of benefits that move beyond the many educational benefits. These benefits are true for all of the children in your home, whether they are yours temporarily or forever.

Reading provides an escape from reality. Whether children are going through something that would be devastating for anyone, including adults, or something that they will most likely not remember into adulthood, children can step away from their current situations and get lost in a book. Problems can feel like a million miles away when you are fighting the supervillain to save the universe or wondering if the prince will even find the kidnapped princess. Even if for a short time, children can forget the problems of their lives and let their imagination take over. As they find themselves lost in the storylines or learning about one of their favorite things, you can see the worry and anxiety start to wash away. This causes a reduction in stress and a reduction in stress leads to better sleeping. The same child we watched scream during the day and cry himself to sleep at night is the same child laughing at a book before bed and peacefully falling asleep.

When children are going through difficult situations, it's sometimes hard to talk to adults. I've found this to be true with our children and students alike. Books provide a way to talk about difficult situations and tough choices without making children feel threatened, embarrassed, or vulnerable. Children can talk about the characters and their experiences without having to discuss their own personal experiences. This can increase communication on what can be tough conversations to have. Reading books about tough situations can also help children know they aren't alone. They become empowered to talk about different situations. No matter their background, every child will face tough choices and difficult situations in life. Characters provide a window to talk through things like right and wrong, positive and negative consequences, feelings, etc. Seeing how characters persevere through challenging times and deal with both positive and negative consequences of their behavior help build children's confidence and optimism in dealing with their personal situations. Children can be motivated and encouraged through the stories of others.

So much of the success of children can be traced back to the relationships they have in their lives. As a literacy coach, I encourage all educators to foster a community with positive and strong relationships inside schools. I've seen the benefits of these types of relationships in the academic setting time and time again.

The culture in a school is powerful. I also know how important these relationships are outside of the classroom as well. It doesn't take research to know that successful people had and continue to have positive role models in their lives. This book is full of people sharing about those who positively shaped the successful people they are today. In my experiences as a mother, both biological and foster, I have seen the effect of building strong, positive relationships. I'm sure many of us have heard of, or experienced, children who don't love to read. If you have, you have seen how this can affect them academically. We all know that there are lifelong benefits to reading, including memory improvement and an increased level of intelligence. We want children to continue to read throughout life because we know if they "don't use it, they'll lose it." We want them to be productive and successful citizens of the community. We want them to have a lifelong love of reading. I've seen this happen with children in my home. Through the positive shared experiences, I've seen children learn that there is so much to gain from reading. Whether you want to be entertained or learn about something that makes you curious, there is an internal fire of desire that begins to light when you get excited about reading. The more you read, the more you want. Some of this is also the example my husband and I set when we read. Their curiosity blooms as to why we want to read so much. If adults want to do it, it must be something interesting!

It took seeing the drastic changes in some of the children who have come into our home temporarily to see the added benefits to reading that move beyond the classroom setting. Whether you are a parent, foster parent, grandparent, aunt, godparent, or more, I hope that you consider these added benefits when it comes to the children in your lives.

―――――――――――

Lindsey Kistner is an elementary school literacy coach with Chesterfield County Public Schools in Virginia.

Learning Through Play

by Kay Starke

As a young girl growing up in Southwest Virginia, my childhood memories revolved around play. We were always outside ….running, playing, riding bikes, exploring the neighborhood, and on rainy days, we were inside playing board games and card games, we were reading and singing and playing with dolls and paper dolls. There was no schedule to follow or activities to attend…..we had FUN everyday just PLAYING. Even when the school year started, we would take advantage of the two hours of outside play at the end of our school day.

I have always loved children. The path I have chosen in life has always revolved around the young child. My college major is in Early Childhood Education. I worked as a nanny, a lifeguard, a recreation supervisor, a coach, a religion teacher, and I have taught in the preschool field for over thirty years.

I am also a parent to three daughters. I think back about their idyllic childhood and how they also played "creatively" throughout their childhood. They ran restaurants, started businesses, they played school, they used mathematic skills as they designed homes, and engineering skills as they built with blocks and legos. Their social skills were evident as they interacted with each other and their friends. They learned to share, and their conversational skills were outstanding. My three daughters are accomplished, smart, educated, well-adjusted, independent women, and their childhood centered around play.

For parents of today, I like to stress the importance of "play is learning." It has been said "a child's play is their work." Educating the parent is the key. During our orientation with parents, I tell them your child is receiving "academic" learning throughout the day. When we sing nursery rhymes, we are leaning about word families; when your child recognizes labels in the store of cereal boxes and crackers, those are pre-reading skills; and when they recognize a STOP sign and a McDonalds sign, they are reading words. When we sing, we are repeating words and using our memorization skills. In our group time while I read a story, the children use their problem-solving ability as they answer who, what , when, and where questions. The children are learning in a fun way and they are prepared for kindergarten.

I saw a bumper sticker recently that read "...READ SING PLAY.....a child's mind cannot wait." Reading, singing, exploring, and playing with your young child has been proven to be an essential part of a child's educational success and has a lifetime of benefits as they continue to grow. My wish is for children of today is to have the fun, play-filled childhood that me and my children have experienced over the years and that the world will once again stress to parents and educators that a child's play is their work.

"We don't stop playing because we grow old, we grow old because we stopped playing." George Bernard Shaw

---

Kay Starke *received her degree in Early Childhood Education. She has taught kindergarten and has been teaching in the preschool field for over 30 years. She presently serves as the Curriculum/Resource Coordinator at a Preschool Center. Kay is married and lives in Richmond, Virginia with her husband Jay. They have three daughters and one granddaughter.*

A Love of Reading: From Generation to Generation

by Marcus J. Newsome, Ed.D.

As a child, I was an unapologetic daydreamer. It gave me boundless satisfaction spending countless hours in school and at home gazing out the window, daydreaming about all kinds of adventures and of life's mysteries. Some of the books we read in school often served as the inspiration for my mental exploits and escapades. In my hometown, classical literature was a prominent part of our school curriculum. However, as far back as the first grade, I can remember the genre that captured my imagination most was Aesop's Fables. Aesop was a storyteller believed to have lived in Ancient Greece between 620 and 564 BC.

Aesop's Fables are written in short story format and seemed to appeal to me because the themes were typically humorous tales of entertaining animals who acted and talked while maintaining their animal traits. And there was also a moral to the story with which I could identify. Childhood lessons learned from Aesop's Fables, classical literature, comic books, and other forms of literature were the foundation for my education career that includes four college degrees and service as an educator for over three decades. Metaphors, figurative language, and parables were important concepts for my foundation as a critical thinker, problem solver, innovator, and lifelong learner.

My love for learning has been passed down to my children and to my children's children. As it is the tradition for some families to eat dinner together every night, so was it a tradition for my wife and I to set aside family time every night to read with our children—7:00 p.m. every night, to be precise. Perhaps this is the reason our oldest child started her own book club when she was a young elementary school student. I can remember her robust home library and her joy of trading books with her classmates as they completed one novel after another.

Now her love for reading has been passed down to her children. She and her husband have given my wife and me two grandsons. She started reading to her own children while she was still pregnant with each of them. Once they were born, I showered them with books at every opportunity. Our family has perpetuated a new generation of children who love books. And I have no doubt that our grandsons will pass their love for reading on to their children, from generation to generation.

―――――――――――

Dr. Marcus J. Newsome completed his 10th year as superintendent of Chesterfield County Public Schools (Virginia), one of the nation's 100 largest school districts. Under his leadership the system has been transformed into a national model for high-performing school districts. Previously he was employed as superintendent of Newport News Public Schools where all high schools were ranked by Newsweek magazine as among America's best. Dr. Newsome has served as a consultant to members of Congress, several governors, state and local elected officials, national and international business leaders, and several universities. He also serves on numerous boards and foundations.

Part 5

Celebrity Reader Huddle

Goodnight Little One

by Ashton Shepherd -
copyright 2016

Good night little one it is time for you to rest.
So tomorrow you can wake up feeling your very best!
Snuggle up inside soft covers tucked in nice and snug.
Now the night has softly fallen with moonlight
shining from above.
Watch the trees against the window blowing in the breeze.
Listening closely to this story your loved one quietly reads.
Your little eyes will soon be heavy as you drift off to dream,
Of adventurous lands, diamond filled skies,
and all you wish to make believe.
Tomorrow holds a sunny morn with lots of fun and play.
Falling asleep means waking up to another special day.
Now I lay me down to sleep and with bedtime prayers all done.
Out like a light shining so bright,
And then a kiss...Goodnight little one.

Background Behind The Poem: Ashton wrote this poem hoping to have it chosen to be part of the Literacy Project for the book #TACKLE READING. "I placed myself in the role of the child going to sleep as well as the role of the mother/father/loved one who would be reading this to their child. I love to read and thankfully, so do my children. My son, James is 10 now. He started reading in Kindergarten. My daughter, Raden is 4 and she is starting to read now and can trace her letters very well and color inside the lines. They are both very smart children and I owe a lot of that to reading books, poems and even songs." As a county music established singer/songwriter, Ashton writes songs every day and plays along with her guitar. "My children were brought up listening to music, going on the road with me and seeing my shows. Music is continuously around them. They even try to write their own songs too," smiles Ashton. "They are both super talented children and I encourage them and every child out there to read and never give up."

Ashton Shepherd: Billboard hot country artist Ashton Shepherd brings her authentic country southern sound to her current album, This Is America. This southern Alabama country girl's previous chart-topping hits include Sounds So Good, Takin' Off This Pain, Where Country Grows, and her Top 20 country hit Look It Up. She is a wonderful wife and mother to two children. "I am a singer/songwriter and I would love to further my career in many outlets that I have ideas about! I do my best to be a Momma and a wife first because that's the best job in the world! It can be sometimes hard to find the balance. I am all about giving my children the best education possible.

Facebook: www.facebook.com/AshtonShepherd (over 90k likes) Twitter: www.twitter.com/ashton_shepherd (over 3k followers) Instagram: http://instagram.com/AshtonShepherdOfficial

Books and Looks

by Veronica Grey

I have always been quiet and kept to myself unless someone drew me out of my shell. It doesn't mean I don't enjoy a good party. But I definitely could wander in and out of one for a couple of hours, enjoying the music, dancing, laughing, having an absolutely fabulous time, but not actually having a real meaningful connection with anyone.

On my 13th birthday, an intuitive neighbor gave me a diary so that I could capture all my feelings and put them in writing. Maybe that's what turned me into somewhat of a teenage recluse. Instead of watching television, I spent hours and hours of my formative years journaling and devouring books. And surfing.

At the age of 18 I got accepted into UCLA as an English major. Literature consumed me (along with playing Lacrosse). When I graduated, I went backpacking all over Europe. What was supposed to last only 3 months ended up being 21 months of nonstop adventures. I kept in touch with friends with detailed emails and they INSISTED I put all my stories in a book because they were that interesting.

Now if it had been only one friend who suggested I do this, I may never have had that fire lit underneath me to write, but the insistence came from pretty much every person who got to know me on more than just a superficial level so I took their suggestions seriously.

But I had no idea where to begin until a friend pointed out that "All the greats started out self-published. Even Mark Twain was self-published when you think about it."

With so many cookie cutter templates on the Internet today where you basically type in whatever you want and out comes a book (it is THAT easy), I was on my way!!! If you are curious which platform I now prefer since I have tried a few, I find CreateSpace, which distributes through Amazon, the most friendly and lucrative.

I remember the feeling I had when my first (self) published book came out. To hold it in my hands felt like a newborn baby that I had grown in my womb and lovingly delivered.

My friend and I walked up and down every book store on Haight Street San Francisco asking to see if they would carry my books on consignment. All I need is one store to consider myself a legitimately published author, I thought, as I trudged up and down the street with my uber enthusiastic friend. I mean, who cares if you've published if no one reads it???

One store after another rejected me for some reason or another.

"Your book is too avante-garde for our audience."

"We only accept titles from major publishing houses."

"We have reached our capacity for consignment at this time."

The excuse varied but the feeling of being shut down was the same after each time we exited a book store.

On a whim, I thought we should try City Lights Bookstore even though it wasn't on Haight Street (easily walking distance from my apartment) because it was so big and famous that maybe they had room for all authors. And you know what, they DID! They signed my books up immediately and placed like three on their shelves and three in stock.

OMG I WAS PUBLISHED AND MY BOOK WAS FOR SALE! It was literally "that easy."

And on pretty much NO BUDGET. Just good old sweat equity.

Since then I have come a long way with four #1 bestsellers on Amazon. My books have gotten me interviewed so frequently on TV that I am now the world's most televised surfer, branded by the media as "The Queen of Surfing." Because my books (and looks) all help the human race, Harvard crowned me "Supermodel Activist of the Decade."

As I've played the game, I did try hard to get with a "big agency." I dropped quite a bit of money shopping my books around in New York agencies in person and I would love for that to have manifested.

However, in today's day and age of the Information

Superhighway, it is silly not to realize that one can earn a perfectly good income as an independently self-published author. I am living proof. Best of all, once you write a book, it makes you money FOREVER. You "work once" and see money automatically appear in your bank account in perpetuity because that's how online sales are set up.

Some of my favorite lessons growing up in high school AP English class include, "Tighten, Brighten, and Sharpen" when it comes to writing. Basically that means that throw out any unnecessary words = tighten.

Use alliterative words that sound nice together and sing together = brighten (i.e., Lucy loves lemonade).

Finally, choose your words carefully = sharpen.

I'll always remember these nuggets of wisdom from my high school AP English class.

Whenever I think about literacy or the lack of it, rather than feeling pity for the individual, I try to feel empathy because no one likes pity. I imagine their lives must be like mine when I am in another country like Greece and can't really understand what the signs say. When I order from the menu, I pray I am getting something I want to eat.

If you are going to read and write, and do it for a living, you may as well reach for the top and be an international bestseller. There is a lady I have worked with, SandiMasori@gmail.com who has a 100% success rate with taking any writer with any book to #1 on Amazon. Some companies charge five figures for such a publicity campaign but hers cost a mere fraction of that, especially if you tell her Veronica Grey sent you.

If a kid like me could get to the top of this game, so can you! All you have to do is press play and believe in yourself and stop at nothing. Dozens of record companies turned down The Beatles before they finally got signed. Always keep going. Never give up. All you need is ONE!

Veronica Grey
Documentarian of the Year
http://worldfilmawards.org/worlddocumentaryawards/winners_wda.htm

My Way Within Words

by Bobby Long

I was first drawn to the power of reading and words by my father's collection of Spike Milligan books. Spike Milligan was a comedian and writer from the 1950s to the 2000s who wrote both the material for his television sketch shows and books of varying natures. It was his books and poems for children, most notably *A Children's Treasury of Milligan*, that took me away to a magical place. This book involved great drawings and poems about imaginary lands, funny characters, and silly wordplay that had me bent over in stitches as a young kid. While silly and funny, this was the first time I had experienced poetry outside of the tight confines of an upper class accent and a distant ancient language I did not understand. For example:

> *My Sister Laura*
> *My sister Laura's bigger than me,*
> *and lifts me up quite easily.*
> *I can't lift her, I've tried and tried;*
> *She must have something very heavy inside.*
> *--Spike Milligan*

It was then that I found my world had changed. I had found the Third Realm. For me, the first and second ones involved the outdoors and TV and film. The Third Realm that I had wandered into had me entranced and involved the written word, a hard copy of a book, and my endless imagination. The power and beauty of words had never been clear to me before. I'm dyslexic, and while I enjoyed reading in the past, the simplicity of poetry was especially easy for me to understand; and I loved that, upon further exploration, poetry could be funny, deeply personal, historical, and entirely creative. Summed up with a sentence or ten stanzas.

I had previously found reading extremely difficult. Looking down the spine of a thick book was a long and challenging task for me, especially due to my learning difficulty. It was through my own exploration and looking up authors and poets connected to a particular writer that I found my own personal tastes, similarly to how I found my musical favorites. I was first exposed to The Beatles and, from them, found my way all the way to the genre of country music and to hip hop by my own musings. While I pushed myself to read Dostoyevsky and other great Russian authors, I fell in love with the simplicity and short stories of Ernest Hemingway, Albert Camus, and Jorge Luis Borges. *The Book of Sand* (by Borges) opened my eyes to the power of short stories and helped broaden my attention span while fluttering my imagination.

While studying for my school exams at 16, I was really disenchanted with the subject of English. All of the books that were a part of the curriculum, that is, *The Handmaid's Tale* and way too much Shakespeare, bored me. I stopped reading so much in my spare time, and I forgot about my Third Realm. That all quickly changed with a school trip to a poetry reading in Bristol, England. I went with my friends, and for the first half of the poetry reading, I sat at the back of this big theatre, chatting away and disinterested in the poetry on offer. We went out for lunch, and my friends decided to not come back, but rather to play hooky and skive. Not being as confident and not wanting to cause trouble, I ran back to the theatre, making it just in time for the second act before my teacher noticed, and I had to sit in the front row because all the other seats were taken. Up stepped a poet called John Cooper Clarke, and I was spellbound, just like I was by Spike Milligan when I was younger. Clarke, a punk poet, rattled off his poems like Eminem and spoke about drugs, poverty in Northern England (where I was born), and emitted great comedy and street slang that I could relate to. I was hooked again. It was also due to him that I started to open up to the other poets who spoke after him. Poets like Simon Armitage, the current Professor of Poetry at Oxford University, Britain's second-most-prestigious literary position after poet laureate, whom I still read to this day.

I was fortunate to have a wonderful English teacher called Mrs. Mills. She was able to see my passion for poetry and reading and gave me a book by Dylan Thomas that completely sealed my lifetime love of words. I had never appreciated the importance of a teacher until that moment. I felt supported and have continued to do so by her enthusiasm and the extra lengths that she went to as a result of noticing my quiet love, which has been the backbone of my creative life so far.

I have since gone on to become a touring musician and songwriter, and I am about to release my second book of poetry. I can't explain the good that writing and reading has done for my own personal mental health. Reading about someone's own experiences, no matter how trivial, is reassuring, relatable, and valuable. I feel more a part of the human race, and the happy isolation I have achieved through reading is meditative and my happy place. Being able to write down my thoughts, feelings, and my stupid ideas is equally as important to me. Whether it's writing a poem or writing daily in your diary, it's not only fun but the very expression brings you closer to what is going on around you and your place within it.

––––––––––––

Bobby Long is a British singer, songwriter, and poet who was born in Wigan in England's industrial north and grew up in the pastoral countryside of Wiltshire. He moved to London to attend university, where he studied music for film. It was there that he found his voice as a musician and songwriter, emerging from the burgeoning club scene with a reputation for creating memorable songs inhabited by hauntingly poetic lyrics. Relix Magazine described him as "He's more Dylan Thomas than Bob Dylan." Since relocating to New York in 2009, he has produced three full albums and an EP of compelling original material as well as a book of poetry. His second volume of poetry will be released later this year (2016).

Visit: www.bobbylong.info
www.musicbobbylong.com
https://twitter.com/BobbyLongNews
www.facebook.com/musicbobbylong
www.youtube.com/musicbobbylong

Dolly Parton's Imagination Library

'I've always been a dreamer, and dreams are special things.
But dreams are of no value if they're not equipped with wings.
Secure yourself for climbing, make ready for the sky.
Don't let your chance go by; you'll make it if you try.'

As a little girl growing up poor in a very rural area of Sevier County, Tennessee, Dolly Parton didn't have books in her home. One of twelve children, Dolly and her siblings often slept three and four in a bed in their one-room cabin. Though she often describes her dad as one of the wisest men she has ever known, he was functionally illiterate, unable to read and write, and she watched him struggle with literacy his entire life. Their family held on to hope and grateful hearts, but times were tough. Yet even as a little girl, Dolly had big dreams. She let her imagination soar far beyond the Smoky Mountain foothills as she sat in her mother's lap listening to her tell stories from the Bible. She chased these dreams all the way to Nashville and, with amazing talent, an embrace of hard work, and a little luck, Dolly became a star.

'Nothing is impossible if you can just believe.
Don't live your life in shackles when faith can be your key.
The winner's one who keeps determination in his eyes.
Who's not afraid to fly and not afraid to try.'

While Dolly went on to become a successful country music and film star, she never forgot her experiences as a little girl. In fact, she used them as inspiration to pursue another of her big dreams - creating a way to ensure that no child had to grow up without books in their home. In 1995, Dolly created the Imagination Library to inspire in children a love of books and reading early in life.

As it has since inception, Dolly Parton's Imagination Library program mails a high-quality, age-appropriate book once a month directly to the homes of registered children from birth to age five. The books are specially selected by a panel of educators, academics, and early childhood specialists according to the age of the receiving child. They progress in complexity and themes to assist in developing skills along the way. For example, books for infants and one-year-olds have minimal text and target vision, touch, rhyme, and rhythm while books for the four-to-five age range move into topics such as diversity, appreciation, handling emotions, and conflict and resolution. The book formats progress from board books to soft cover, and a majority of the books have title-specific reading tips helping parents and caregivers engage the child and enhance the reading time. The books are always free to the family and arrive at the home with a special label addressing the book with the child's name on it.

Through the Dollywood Foundation, Dolly initially provided the gift of books only to children in her hometown of Sevier County, Tennessee. During this initial period, the effort received numerous awards and extraordinary national media attention. Soon interest poured in from communities across the country desiring to have the Imagination Library for their children. For the program to grow beyond Sevier County, Tennessee, it needed a structure that would allow it to be easily adopted and sustained by any community. With much thought and creative planning, Dolly's team devised a unique partnership model that would allow exactly that. In the year 2000, Dolly announced that she would make her Imagination Library available for replication in any community that would support it locally.

The unique partnership model has seen remarkable success. In 2004 the governor of Tennessee, joined by Dolly, announced the first statewide Imagination Library program and established the infrastructure that made the program available to all 400,000+ preschool children in the state. The program continued to gain international attention, expanding to Canada in 2007, United Kingdom in 2008, and Australia in 2014. With over 1,500 communities taking advantage of the opportunity and thousands of local volunteers working to make the Imagination Library available in their communities, the program now mails over 925,000 books each month. To date, Dolly's Imagination Library program has mailed over 78 million books to children across the U.S.A., Canada, the United Kingdom, and Australia. In addition, more than 1.6 million children have turned five and "graduated" from the program better prepared for success in school and life.

'The path you're taking now can make a difference.
It all depends on just how hard you try.'

So, books are great, but why does all of this matter? While for most there is an intuitive understanding as to why it is a good idea for children to have books when they are growing up, the importance of this simple act goes much deeper than that. We all know that when a child loves something, the child will continue to do it, and the Imagination Library has a lot to do with the emotional tie to books. The books are specially selected to excite the imagination and develop a love of reading, and getting one-on-one attention from a caregiver can deeply instill the significance of time together with a great book. Also, do you remember getting your own mail when you were a child? It was a big deal. When children realize they are receiving their very own piece of mail with their name on it, their ownership of the books increases even more.

It is also important to know that in the first three to four years of a child's life, brain development for motor skills, language skills, and higher cognitive function is at its peak. Reading, talking, and singing regularly with a child from birth is one of the best ways a parent can help stimulate language and literacy development in a child. The Imagination Library makes sure that families and children have stimulating, age-appropriate books to help drive this interaction. There is a considerable amount of research showing that families who receive Imagination Library books read more often together among other things, ultimately helping the children be better prepared to learn when they arrive at school.

The simple act of sitting down and reading age-appropriate books with a child has a tremendous impact on the life. Further, the Imagination Library has proven to be a great foundation for many complementary supports that a community may put in place to foster family literacy and prepared children. So look for Dolly Parton's Imagination Library in your community and support local efforts aimed at developing healthy, prepared children. Most importantly, start by grabbing a great book and reading with a child.

> *'The first step is the one that's always hardest.*
> *But nothing's gonna change if you don't try.*
> *So spread your wings and let the magic happen.*
> *You'll never really know unless you try.*

(Lyrics to 'Try' by Dolly Parton)

Jeff Conyers
Executive Director, The Dollywood Foundation
www.imaginationlibrary.com

Reading Through My Eyes

by Ed Lucas

As a journalist, best-selling author, and broadcaster, people ask me what it takes to be a writer.

There are many answers, of course, but the most important one is to read, read some more, and read even more after that.

Good readers become strong writers, and they also make the best storytellers.

In 1949, when I was ten years old, my Mom bought me a paperback called Bat Boy of The Giants, a first person account by Garth Garreau of his days as a teenager assisting the baseball players of the New York (now San Francisco) Giants in the clubhouse and on the field. I fell in love with it. I devoured all 206 pages of that book from cover to cover numerous times. I still have the book. It's dog eared and tattered, but a nice reminder of the thrill that learning to read gave me in my boyhood days.

My goal was to become a Giants bat boy like Garth, or maybe even a player for them someday.

Those dreams were shattered in 1951, when I went out to play baseball with my friends and a line drive smacked me right between the eyes.

That was the last thing I ever saw.

There are many things a twelve-year-old boy longs to do. Lying in a hospital bed afraid of living life as a helpless blind person is not one of them.

Many people, even well meaning ones, told me that my life was over. They said that disabled folks were limited and had no future, especially one in baseball. All I thought I'd be good for was standing on a corner with a tin cup and a cane begging for pennies.

Luckily, I had faith, family, and friends to get me through the darkness.

My Dad and Mom sat by my bedside every day for three months, praying and reading anything they could to me – including *Bat Boy of the Giants* – to lift my spirits.

My mother went even further, reaching out to the biggest baseball stars of the day, telling them my story. They responded in an amazing way. Legends like Joe DiMaggio, Willie Mays, Stan Musial, and Ted Williams all got in touch with me personally and encouraged me to never give up on my dreams and to turn my passion for and knowledge of baseball into a career as a writer or broadcaster.

The most surprising response of them all was from New York Yankees MVP and future Hall of Famer Phil "The Scooter" Rizzuto. My mom took me to meet him at a clothing store near our house where he worked during the offseason (the players didn't make as much money back then as they do today.) They all had to have other jobs.

Scooter became a close friend and mentor, urging me to ignore the doubters and to get a good education. I did just that, graduating with a degree in communications from Seton Hall University in New Jersey. Even then, the road wasn't smooth.

Discrimination against the disabled was commonplace in the early 1960s. Many veteran reporters and players didn't want a blind person in the clubhouse. They tried hard to keep me out. I didn't let them discourage me. Instead, I studied their writing. I read their articles and books, which gave me a better idea of what it took to cover ballgames on the major league level. Eventually, my persistence paid off and I began a career that has lasted for six decades.

I've been blessed to have a best-selling book of my own, to be honored as a journalist, and to win an Emmy Award for my work on television.

I consider my greatest accomplishment in life, however, to be raising my two boys, Eddie and Chris. Both of them are grown men now and have sons of their own. They are passing the love of reading along to the next generation, just as I did for them.

That was quite a challenge for me at first.

One of the joys of being a parent is sitting down at your child's bedside and reading a goodnight story. My Dad did it for me, but since I couldn't see words on the page, it was difficult for me to do for Eddie and Chris.

One night, when he was six, Eddie called me into his room. It was long past his bedtime, but he was full of energy. He wanted me to read to him from his favorite Disney storybook. I desperately wanted to, but couldn't. I offered to recite a fairy tale for Eddie from memory, but he was insistent. He handed me the book, wanting to read along with his father. I was trying to come up with another way to satisfy his request, but nothing worked. It was very frustrating and sad for both of us.

A few months later, I found a company called Twin Vision for the Blind that provided free Braille books for blind parents to read along with their children. I signed up. The night the first book - *Pinocchio* - arrived, I sat down on the edge of Eddie's bed and cried as I read it side by side with him.

Like the little puppet in the story, a transformation occurred. A whole new world had opened up for both of us. To Eddie, I wasn't his "blind" father, I was just "Daddy."

There were no more "strings" on me. You can shed yours, too.

Each of us in life will face challenges and limitations at one point. Mine is a huge one, the inconvenience of not having sight. Yours might be less severe, but still enough of an obstacle to make you stop in your tracks.

Luckily, there's a way over and around even the greatest road blocks, and that's by reading.

The answers to any dilemma can be found in your local library or bookstore. No matter what you are going through, someone has gone through it before. They have also written down their experiences. Their words reach across generations and through time to enrich and uplift us, no matter our age or reading level.

A life spent reading is a life fully lived. I know this from my personal experience.

While I never did get to be the bat boy of the Giants, thanks to reading I actually got to follow in the footsteps of giants instead. That same opportunity is there for you if you embrace your curiosity and read, even just a little bit, each and every day of your life.

I wish you many blessings on your lifelong journey as a reader. I'm confident that by sharpening this skill, you will be a great success in whatever you choose to do.

Ed Lucas is an Emmy Award-winning broadcaster who has been covering professional sports since 1955, despite being totally blind. A member of three different Halls of Fame, Ed travels the world as a motivational speaker. He and his wife, Allison, live in New Jersey. EdLucasOnline.com

How My Love Of Reading Changed My Life

by Patrenna Singletary

Believe it or not, I did not know I was in love with reading until I was approached by my sixth grade teacher about playing Mrs. Santa Claus in the upcoming school play. I had never done any acting before and the role called for me to sing as well. I was a very shy, quiet, mild mannered little girl who did not like a lot of attention. By accepting this lead role in the school play, it would take me completely out of my comfort zone. She also advised me to pursue a career as an anchorperson on the news. This was the beginning of not only my career in the public eye but also a chance to escape to another world through reading.

I began to read fashion magazine articles and imagine myself in the fashion industry with all of the glamour and beautiful attire. I dreamed of living the lifestyle of the rich and famous, a celebrity signing autographs and accepting awards as an actress... even practicing my Academy Awards speech. The funny thing about it was in my mind I could envision myself doing this, but my shyness quickly overtook me and returned me to reality. The more and more I read not only just fashion magazines, but books like *Great Expectations* and other coming-of-age novels, I knew I needed to release the shyness, but I did not know how. As a result, I developed a persona, a role, or character I could easily transition into in order to perform the task at hand with confidence. Utilizing my persona gave me the ability to reach for the stars and finally escape into the world that I knew I could be a part of! As a result, I was able to master the role of Mrs. Santa Claus and the singing that was required of me. I felt a sense of accomplishment that ultimately became second nature as other roles presented themselves throughout my primary school years. I was able to join the Glee Club in middle school, and at the high school level compete in regional Theatre and Drama tournaments, narrate a compelling documentary on the Memphis City Schools Guidance Counseling Program for the Public Broadcasting Station (PBS), several local television appearances and hosted my very own weekly FM radio station segment about my high school. All of these achievements at such an early age would have never transpired if it had not been for the love of reading and allowing myself to become engrossed in the adventures to the point where I too felt I could become successful.

To this day, this is how I view my love of reading as an escape! I owe a great deal of gratitude to my sixth-grade teacher because she not only introduced me to the joy of reading for performances but also opened the door to my career in broadcasting. Although I was not quite sure what she was referring to when she told me about being an anchorperson on the news, it captured my interest and I automatically knew there would be some reading involved. As we all know, being able to read effectively and to articulate this information to the general public is a skill that can only be acquired through reading with comprehension. Truth be told, when I finally researched and understood the role of an anchorperson on the news, the more I could actually see myself being one.... that is with the help of my persona. I liked watching the news with my Dad and I vividly remember admiring the news team and saying to myself: "That is going to be me one day!" I loved the professionalism of it all coupled with the fact that they were on television and they were always welcomed into your homes daily. At that time, I did not know they were reading teleprompters. When I found out about the reading component, I just knew this career goal was a match made in heaven for me! I would practice in the mirror reading makeshift news stories with a look of concern, yet professionalism just so I could say: "Now Back To You....(whomever)! Those were fun times for me and I will never forget them.

Although after my formative years ended and I began my college education, I majored in Organizational Management and Leadership, not Broadcast Journalism or Communications as I originally thought I would pursue. Nonetheless, I was able to utilize my reading comprehension skills in a number of other ways in the corporate arena, the education industry and through nonprofit philanthropic efforts. I was still able to achieve a great deal within those entities through awards, meaningful collaborations, and helping college students to reach their professional potential which I later coined the term: "Edutainment" due to the fact that I carefully maneuvered my entertainment skills into my career as a college educator in an effort to be creative in reaching my students and it worked! As I implemented this edutainment procedure, I began to notice that my students began to gravitate more toward reading their assignments as I had done so long ago. It had all come back full circle for me....I had become my sixth-grade teacher to my own students. This was the crowning achievement for me!

I will always value my years as an Educator and being able to "Pay It Forward" as it pertains to my love of reading! As I now reap the rewards of being back in the entertainment industry with the Singletary Network NY and the Michael D. Singletary Foundation, which is devoted to helping students reach their full professional potential, I know first hand that reading works! I am a firm believer that had I not developed the love of reading, I would not be able to do what I am doing now!

I am very proud to be a part of the Tackle Reading movement and I encourage others to help children explore brave new worlds through reading. You never know how this will impact their lives for many years to come! I dedicate this story to my sixth-grade teacher, Mrs. Wiley at Carnes Elementary School in Memphis, TN! Who would have thought this shy, little, wimpy kid would develop the where with all to pursue her dreams in the Edutainment industry? You did Mrs. Wiley....You did....and I am forever grateful to you, I salute you!

———————

Patrenna is the President and CEO of The Singletary Network NY and The Chairperson of The Michael D. Singletary Foundation. She is a firm believer in education, especially reading. She has served in various positions within Corporate America with such noted companies as the Federal Express Corporation, Federal Ex Services World Technology Headquarters, International Paper, The Conwood Company, LLP, Leader Federal Bank For Savings, and a number of other companies. She has also enjoyed a lucrative career in the education arena as the Business Department Chair for National College Memphis whereas she headed the Business Management, Logistics Supply Chain Management and Accounting departments. She pursued a career in entertainment at a very early age which blossomed into a global Internet -based media company, The Singletary Network NY which houses stellar radio programs with Celebrities, New York Times Best Selling Authors, Grammy and Tony Award Winners, Subject Matter Experts, and Every Day Business Professionals. Her global network broadcasts on iHeartRadio, Blogtalkradio, iTunes, The Women's Radio Network, and Beasley Media\ CBS Radio! She provides quality REAL LIFE programming devoted to select markets: Nashville Presents: Saturdays with Singletary and Atlanta Presents: Simply Singletary are two of the shows she hosts personally.

Part 6

Reading and Writing Is My Life in the End Zone

Never Give Up

by DM Jack

When I was young, I had a terrible reading problem. In fact, I had a second-grade reading level in fifth grade on top of dyslexia, which wasn't caught until my home room teacher finally brought it to my parent's attention. This situation arose in the public school system of a wealthy town, not an inner city school with limited resources, so it can happen to anyone. At the time, the school had the resources to work with students challenged by the curriculum, but this was many years ago before programs for learning disabilities such as dyslexia existed.

After completing elementary school, I was tested (I failed miserably) and sent to a special school that worked with kids that had reading disabilities (and unfortunately related behavioral problems). It took me three years to catch up and an additional year at prep school to get back to my grade level.

In eleventh grade, an amazing teacher came into my life and catapulted me beyond my perceived limitations. He was a college -level professor who chose to teach high school boys, not only English but important study habits, discipline, and life lessons. He was the hardest teacher in the school and rarely gave out an "A." He taught us the classics and made us stretch our minds. He would ask the class open-ended questions with subjective answers to build our analytical skills.

One day after class, he approached me with a homework paper I had just handed in the day before. It was my response to a question that had no right or wrong answer. I was afraid that my opinion made no sense and was fully expecting a poor grade. Instead, he wrote on the top of the page, "Incredible Statement," and I received an "A" for the first time in that school!

This was a turning point in my education and literally changed my perspective about who I was and my abilities. From that moment on, with hard work and persistence, I was an "A" student. I graduated in the top ten of my class and minored in English in college. Ultimately, my weakness became my strength. I specialized in business communications and sales during a long career in media and advertising and now write books and screenplays – but it all starts with reading comprehension.

- If you're having a problem with reading and don't understand the lesson, don't be afraid to tell your parents and ask for help.

- It's okay and doesn't mean you're stupid. In fact, you are smart for bringing it to their attention.

- I didn't tell anyone about my reading problem for years and was moved through each grade without understanding valuable fundamentals in the process.

- Teachers don't always catch these issues and kids can fall through the cracks of the system. So parents, if you suspect a problem, arrange a meeting with the teacher. The quicker the issue is dealt with and resolved, the better for everyone – most importantly your child.

- Reading and writing is fundamental to success in all aspects of life. If you do your best, never give up and believe in yourself, you can do anything, including becoming an author and teaching others what you have learned.

Good luck!

David

_____

*by **DM Jack** Author, Founder & President Sightline Media Entertainment LLC*

Making Facts Fun: Using Nonfiction in the Classroom

by John Micklos, Jr.

Nonfiction is the Rodney Dangerfield of children's book genres. Like the famed comedian, it just doesn't get any respect. Even its name reflects that—it's "not fiction." But times are changing, and in recent years nonfiction is garnering increased attention.

For one thing, the Common Core State Standards place increased emphasis on nonfiction. The standards recommend that reading materials for Grade 4 students be split evenly between fiction and nonfiction. Grade 8 students, the standards say, should be reading 55% nonfiction, and Grade 12 students should be reading 70% nonfiction. That's a seismic change, especially at the elementary level, where just a few years ago fiction comprised the vast majority of students' reading materials.

Furthermore, nonfiction was rated "hot" by three-quarters of the respondents to the 2015 "What's Hot in Literacy" survey conducted by Jack Cassidy and colleagues and published in the International Literacy Association's Literacy Today publication. Why is nonfiction so important for today's students? Here are some key reasons:

- It presents "real world" topics.
- It gives students valuable background knowledge about the world around them.
- It teaches academic vocabulary.
- It helps students make the transition to "reading to learn."
- It prepares them for the materials they will encounter on standardized tests—and in life.

Nonfiction books take many forms: biographies/autobiographies, history, social studies, science, and more. I've written more than 20 nonfiction books for young readers from elementary school through high school, and I can attest that many students find nonfiction just as interesting and engaging as fiction. In fact, for some readers, especially reluctant or challenged readers, factual material may be easier to grasp than the nuances of novels.

What are some of the key factors that make nonfiction books appealing to young readers? Here are some things I look for when writing these books:

Fun facts. On February 14, 1876, rival inventors Alexander Graham Bell and Elisha Gray both submitted patent applications for the telephone. Bell received the patent; Gray didn't. Had things gone differently, Gray would be the famous one.

Anecdotes that illuminate a person's life or a particular event. Long before she became a world-famous pilot, Amelia Earhart built a "roller coaster" in her backyard out of old pieces of lumber. She was a daredevil even at age seven.

Information or quotes that help students understand the context for an event. For instance, when writing a book about the Challenger tragedy, it's important to note that this particular shuttle mission was special because a civilian—teacher Christa McAuliffe—was aboard. Millions of people were watching when the shuttle exploded, and the tragedy seemed magnified by the fact that a teacher was among the seven who died.

What can teachers do to help engage students in nonfiction?

Teach students about the inherent interest of informational texts. Nonfiction texts help us learn important and interesting details about the world around us.

Look for high-interest topics that relate to the curriculum. More than ever, there are a wide variety of high-quality nonfiction books relating to nearly any curricular topic you can imagine.

Look for "far out facts" and amazing statistics. These will captivate young readers and may be especially appealing to reluctant readers.

Look for series. Many publishers prepare series of books around specific topics. If kids like one book in a series, chances are that they might like others as well.

Share snippets of text as read-alouds. Many teachers think of this as a strategy only for introducing fiction, but it can work well for nonfiction as well.

Pair fiction and nonfiction books. This can be a great way to get different perspectives on a topic.

Go beyond books. Nonfiction materials encompass articles, websites, videos, infographics, and more. The more different types of materials teachers present, the better the odds of finding something that will appeal to all of their students.

Teachers can also help students become engaged and effective readers of nonfiction by helping them learn to find the main ideas in text. Along with this, teachers can help students learn how to use nonfiction text features such as heads and subheads, photos and captions, charts and graphs, the table of contents, the glossary, and the index to aid comprehension.

Teachers can also engage students in nonfiction by getting them to write it. Students enjoy learning how to use nonfiction to inform, to instruct, to persuade, and to narrate. When I work with young writers in schools, I offer these nonfiction tips.

Do thorough research. Use multiple sources, and learn how to evaluate whether sources are trustworthy.

Find fun facts, quotes, and stories. These not only make the piece interesting for readers, but they help make the writing process more enjoyable as well. As a writer, I love discovering a great story or quote to share.

Write both to inform and entertain. There's no reason why effective nonfiction writing can't do both.

Remember to revise. Many students love to write. Fewer like to go back and revise. I remind them that revision is an important tool for writers, and I share examples of how my work changes and evolves through multiple drafts.

In conclusion, I encourage educators to remember that nonfiction isn't the ugly duckling among writing genres. The right nonfiction, with the right introduction, can be the beautiful swan that attracts students to read!

––––––––––––

John Micklos, Jr. is the author of more than 25 books for young readers, including poetry, picture books, and, of course, nonfiction. Learn more at www.JohnMicklosWriter.com.

Reading Muscles

by Tom Doyle (pen name Bo Rush)

As parents and teachers know, reading is a skill that is necessary to be successful in school and in life. Reading deficiency is a roadblock that can prevent achievement in all academic subjects.

Unfortunately, every year as a fourth-grade teacher, I see students who, day after day, avoid reading. They start and quickly abandon books other kids are reading – either because of the level of difficulty or unappealing subject matter. These students frequently are boys, and they have become experts at avoiding reading. It's a widespread problem. Boys' reading scores lag girls' scores in the United States and in many countries around the world.

Many of these reluctant readers are involved in sports outside of school. As a former athlete and youth coach, I've used my own interest in sports to connect with them. I've capitalized on their interests by filling my classroom with sports books, magazines, and bookmarked websites. For many boys, these are exactly the types of reading materials that motivate them to read. Their avoidance behavior typically disappears when they can choose from materials that excite them. The bottom line is that boys read more – and their reading skills improve – when they enjoy what they are reading.

I know this is true from my own personal experience. As a boy, I loved sports. And I loved reading about sports. In fact, I refused to read about anything except sports. There weren't many sports books in those days, so I read game programs, trading cards, newspaper sports pages, sports magazines, anything sports-related that I could get my hands on! I cut out pictures of my favorite athletes and taped them all over my bedroom walls. That singular passion resulted in proficient reading skills – skills that transferred to other subjects and genres when I was in high school and college.

That's why I decided to write *BOBBLEHEAD BEATDOWN**, *BASKETBALL BROTHER* and *SOCCER SIDEKICKS* -- for kids who love sports but don't love reading. I want to spark that love of reading in youngsters, particularly those who are struggling to find the right book. I want to use sports to hook them into reading. Just like sports hooked me.

Bo Rush sports books combine fast-paced sports action with everyday issues all kids face. I have included important themes such as teamwork, perseverance, courage, friendship, and responsibility. And the reading level is appropriate for the majority of elementary school students. *SOCCER SIDEKICKS, BASKETBALL BROTHER*, and *BOBBLEHEAD BEATDOWN* are receiving an overwhelmingly enthusiastic response from teachers and students nationwide.

Tom Doyle *is the children's author of Bo Rush Sports Books*
http://www.borushbooks.com

*Check out a sneak peak from Bobblehead Beatdown Look for it in Part 7.

You Can Lead a Horse to Water,
but Can You Make Her Read?

by Gigi Amateau

Surely, we all agree that reading is good and fun for everybody! Human, avian. Canine, feline. Bovine, equine. Is there a species on Earth that wouldn't benefit from listening to a friend read a treasured story?

Few experiences can compare to reading a cherished story to a beloved horse. My perfect afternoon consists of reading a classic or contemporary horse book to my pony, Angel. Reading in the field gives us time together, increases our trust, and makes me a better reader.

Imagine: surrounded by distant whinnying from neighboring fields, taking in the sweet, grassy smell of manure, and shuddering at the soft tickle of horse whiskers on your neck while Miss Pony herself cranes to read over your shoulder.

Try it for yourself! Go on. I'll wait.

(Note: Not to worry, if no equine is on hand. Reading out loud has many proven benefits for dogs, cats, birds, fish, lizards, mice, and hamsters. The tips below guarantee results in most pets and occasionally in feral squirrels, ducks, and prairie otters.)

Once you've caught your horse or sidled up to him in the pasture, you may begin. Start by reading the title, author, and illustrator. Horses will also appreciate if you note the publisher and date of first printing.

Hay! Whoa! What's that, you say? You've never read aloud to a pony! Sounds a bit difficult?

Ah, fair point.

At home you can simply catch your little sister with a lead rope or lasso your baby brother and hitch him to the sofa, grab a book, fluff up a pillow, and flop back into a riveting book. (Warning: Do not attempt to catch or lasso a sibling who is bossier, louder, or toothier than you. Not everyone enjoys being roped into reading. Sad but true.)

Reading to horses does, indeed, require a well-thought plan. Allow me to demystify the three major keys to excellent reading experiences with equines. (Disclaimer: The following tips are warranted to achieve reading success with all breeds except Shetland Ponies, who though small of stature are, in fact, the bossiest, loudest, and toothiest of their species. In eight out of ten trials, only bribing by peppermint correlated with positive reading outcomes or predictable outcomes of any kind, when the trials involved Shetlands.)

1.   The All-Essential Snack. In thousands of global tests, the leading factor as to whether or not a horse or pony will listen to an entire book relates most often to which snacks the human reader offers at the beginning of the story, during the middle, and at the end. Surprisingly, apples do not seem to hold horsey attention for much more than 20 pages, which is an acceptable strategy, if the book you've chosen ends at page 15. If you're hoping to help your horse or pony rack up AR points, you'll need more tempting snacks. Try the brilliant orange and long-admired root vegetable, the carrot. In standardized equine reading tests, carrots have proven more universally appealing and longer lasting than any other treat. In some cases, much as 70 pages of read aloud material per single carrot or six baby carrots.

For particularly new or particularly reluctant equines, you'll need a more aggressive approach to snackage. A little known function of most any book is that of serving tray. (Tip: With peppermint candy at the ready, turn your book flat, cover side up. Place said candy just above the title. Wave said book alongside first the left, then the right horse nostril. Horse nostrils are ginormous, so your friend should detect the treat quickly. You may then begin reading.)

2.   A Great Book. We'll spend the most time discussing title selections, for while sweet and savory treats may help to entice your pony into a calm, open, and steady listening state of mind, the story matters. Take care to select a book that will enchant but not scare your four-hooved little darling (or very large darling). Do be aware that horses have a well-earned reputation of spooking at any new thing within sight. To members of the equus genus, a red umbrella may be just as scary as a black bear. Therefore, it is generally a good idea to avoid horror, mystery, dark fantasy, or any title that aims to frighten, startle, or shock. (Caution: Many stories have surprise endings, which in some breeds, can cause undue alarm and may send your equine friend careening around the pasture due to unexpected plot twists.)

When choosing your equine read aloud title, you must think like your horse. Ask yourself, what does the equine standing before me really want or need in a story? Knowing your pony's likes and dislikes, interests and hobbies can help guide you to just the right book.

Many U.S. horses rarely leave their paddocks unless to walk to the barn or occasionally to travel to a nearby show. Your horse may know little of the world beyond the barn. It is up to you to bring the richness of our diverse and beautiful world to your friend through books. For example, a rural horse will relish hearing about city lights, high-rises, and after-school riding clubs. Try G. Neri's Ghetto Cowboy, a fast-paced story about city horses and concrete cowboys in North Philly. Say you live in Connecticut, where your gelding specializes in dressage (the ballroom dancing of the horse world). Such a fancy horse will revel in hearing you read about the time-honored tradition of the southwest rodeo in Nancy Bo Flood's book of poetry and pictures, Cowboy Up! Ride the Navajo Rodeo. If your mare needs a confidence boost, the book for her might just be Riding Freedom by Pam Munoz Ryan. Set in the mid-1800s, this is a story of following big dreams and never giving up.

(Advisory: If your only choice is to read aloud to a Shetland, experts recommend starting with The Princess and the Pony by Kate Beaton. This picture book stars Princess Pinecone, who aspires to be a warrior. She wants a brave battle horse but instead is given an adorable, chubby farting pony. Let's just say between the pony's flatulence and cuteness, this book will strike a familiar chord in the heart of Shetland ponies.)

3. Love is Patient and Kind. When you begin your read aloud journey with your pony (or dog or cat or fish or bird or snake or little sister, if you have no nearby horse), do so for one reason only: you love her or him very much, and you want to share a good story. Spending a morning or afternoon reading to my Angel makes us both happy because we are together. Sure, she occasionally flicks her long, black tail at me to hurry up and get to the good parts. Yes, she sometimes wanders off at the sad parts, but I keep on reading. She never shows impatience when I mispronounce a word or mistakenly read the same sentence twice in a row. Every now and then, my little mare rests her head on my shoulder and falls asleep. In those times, when a book has worked its peaceful magic over Angel, and she is resting soundly, I keep on reading. Not even a book platter full of peppermints could make me stop.

Gigi Amateau is an author who currently resides in Richmond, Virginia. Come August, Come Freedom, her first work of historical fiction, won the Library of Virginia's People Choice Award for fiction, and was chosen by Bank Street College as a Best Children's Book of the Year and by the Virginia Library Association as a Jefferson Cup Honor book.

Reaching Reluctant Readers

by Kat Spears

Trying to remember a time when I couldn't read is like trying to remember a time when I couldn't breathe. And that's what reading has always been like for me—breathing. I read when I eat, while I brush my teeth…whenever I'm supposed to be doing something else.

Without the irritating distraction of a paying job, I could easily read a book a day. Reading is a way to travel, to visit worlds foreign to my own, and to know what other people are thinking and feeling. Reading encourages me to feel sadness, fear, regret, elation, and romance, to access universal human feelings in a safe and controlled environment.

Now that I'm a published author, I take a certain amount of pride in the fact that I never passed a high school English class. And it was only through the graces of some very generous professors in college that I passed the required English courses to earn a degree.

In a fit of frustration, one of my college professors once asked me why—why?!—if I was obviously able to ace an exam and contribute to classroom discussions, I insisted on being a solid D student. The only explanation I could offer was that while I loved to read, I didn't like being told what to read. And I liked it even less when someone told me how I was supposed to interpret what I read.

To be completely honest, I often felt lost in English classes. I would do the required reading, and when it came time to discuss it in class, felt as if everyone had read a different book from the one I had read. Everyone else seemed to be in perfect agreement about what the author was trying to express or knew what the protagonist felt. My interpretations were always wildly different from those of other people, including and especially the teacher, and so I learned to keep my opinions to myself.

That professor, the one who was so frustrated with me for being a D student, ended up granting me a B for my end of semester grade. Maybe she felt sorry for me. Maybe she just didn't want to face having me as a repeat presence in her class. Either way, I've spent the rest of my adult life endeavoring to deserve that B.

If you told any of my high school or college English teachers that I am now a published author, they probably wouldn't believe you. After all, I don't know the difference between a sentence and a dependent clause, and I couldn't even begin to tell you what a dangling participle is.

As an author I have a copy editor—a very efficient one with an amazing attention to detail. When I review the manuscript edits she sends me I can almost hear the frustration in her typed words as she carefully explains why a passage is grammatically incorrect. And it makes me feel a bit sorry for her. Poor thing. She slogged through who knows how many hours of learning her craft by carefully diagramming sentences (something else I can't do) and studying various style guides to reach a stellar career as an editor with Macmillan. And she's stuck editing the manuscripts of a person who loves to begin sentences with conjunctions, and end them with prepositions. I don't even like commas very much. And semicolons? Forget it. I would never use one of those, though according to the rules of English, I need them occasionally.

Something else I've discovered now that I'm an author is that readers often see meaning in my writings that were never intended. I'm constantly mystified by the meaning people find hidden in my writings. I promise you that any brilliance from me is only occasionally intentional. I'm not even really given a choice about the story or who the character is as a person. Characters arrive fully formed in my mind, and I tell their stories in their voices.

And that's the beautiful thing about books. Any meaning within a work of literature, the reader provides it, not the author. When people ask me about characters in my books—their hopes, fears, and dreams—I can speculate, say what I think, but I can never be absolutely sure. Once I put a character on a page, he doesn't belong to me anymore. He belongs to the reader. I can't control how the reader will interpret my character's actions or words or how he interacts with the world around him.

Every interpretation of a book or story is valid, because every reader brings a different set of life experiences to what they read. Don't let anyone tell you different.

Kat Spears has worked as a bartender, museum director, housekeeper, park ranger, business manager, and painter (not the artistic kind). She holds an M.A. in anthropology, which has helped to advance her bartending career. She lives in Richmond, Virginia and is the author of Sway, Breakaway, *and* The Boy Who Killed Grant Parker.

Building Background Knowledge Before and After Reading

by Kathryn Starke

Have you ever watched a child read the words perfectly in a book and have no understanding or connection to what he or she is reading? This happens far too often and usually because the reader has no background knowledge or previous experiences related to the theme or topic of the text. Imagine how your own brain feels after reading an article on DNA replication without any information on the subject. It may be confusing, overwhelming, and full of terminology that it makes no sense in context. Children can feel this same way when approaching a text for the first time without any knowledge. Childhood experiences increase our schema, which in turn increases our comprehension. How can you fully understand a fictional story of a trip to the farm without visiting a farm or petting farm animals yourself?

The bottom line is that our life experiences contribute to our reading comprehension throughout our life. One day I was teaching third graders a passage entitled "A New Home." I asked the small group members to make a prediction based on the title. These predictions included the mom having a new baby, the dad getting a promotion, the family getting evicted, and the parents getting divorced, which all resulted in a new home. The actual story was about the grandmother moving in with the family, and since she was in a wheelchair they needed to move to a handicapped accessible house. In another instance with the same group, I introduced the title "Jumping In" which led to predictions of jumping in a pool, jumping into a pile of leaves, playing a game of basketball with a jump ball, and jumping in and out of the way of a gun bullet. Again, these responses are based on the child's life as an eight-year-old. The story was actually about a child jumping off a dock into the river for the first time. When kids have a preconceived notion of what the story will be about, their ultimate understanding may be altered. Here are some effective ways to preview a story that activates a child's background knowledge.

- Take a real or virtual field trip to the setting in the text or location to learn about the information in the text.
- Read both fiction and nonfiction books about one topic to gain a broader perspective.
- Ask children (as illustrated in text above) to make a prediction based on the title alone to determine how you as the teacher will teach the text.
- Wrap a book up, then tear away piece by piece for children to use picture clues to make predictions of what they think the story will be about.
- Lead a picture walk, page by page, encouraging the students to "tell a story" (using only picture clues, no word clues).
- Have the students write an I Predict statement either based on the title and/or going on a picture walk. After reading the book, students will reread the statement to confirm the accuracy of the prediction.
- Students use picture clues and background knowledge to create a story word chart before reading of words, phrases, and ideas they think will appear during reading. The teacher records the word, and the story word chart is posted as a reference tool when decoding new or difficult words.

Part 7

Plays Especially for Children

Reading Is...

by Maddie Holmes

Reading can mean something different to everyone, but this is what it means to me. Reading can take you on an adventure! With all the different settings of a book it can take you anywhere whether it's to the beach or to Alaska. All the characters in the book can have different personalities and characteristics that make the book so much fun and adventurous to read. When I read adventure books, my favorite part is that anything can happen. You could go to another state, or even another galaxy! Another thing I love about reading is that it is very relaxing and calming. I like to have a quiet place when I read because it helps me focus on my book. My favorite spot to read is in my cozy, pink chair in my room. Reading can also take your mind off things. If you are stressed out, reading is a great stress reliever! Lastly, I love reading because you get to choose what to do. You get to choose what genre to read. I like realistic fiction and mystery the best. You can also choose what type of book you want to read whether it's a novel or a picture book. Also, you can choose when to read the book. You could read it when you wake up in the morning, you could read it after lunch, or before you go to bed. These reasons are my opinion on what reading is. What does reading mean to you?

Maddie Holmes, fifth grade

I'm a Word Detective!

I look at the picture

I find hidden words

I make the first sound

I slide my finger from beginning to end of the word

I say the word

I read and I read!

Created by Kathryn Starke

I'm a Word Detective!

I look at the picture

I find hidden words

I make the first sound

I slide my finger from beginning to end of the word

I say the word

I read and I read!

Created by Kathryn Starke

I'm a Word Detective!

I look at the picture

I find hidden words

I make the first sound

I slide my finger from beginning to end of the word

I say the word

I read and I read!

Created by Kathryn Starke

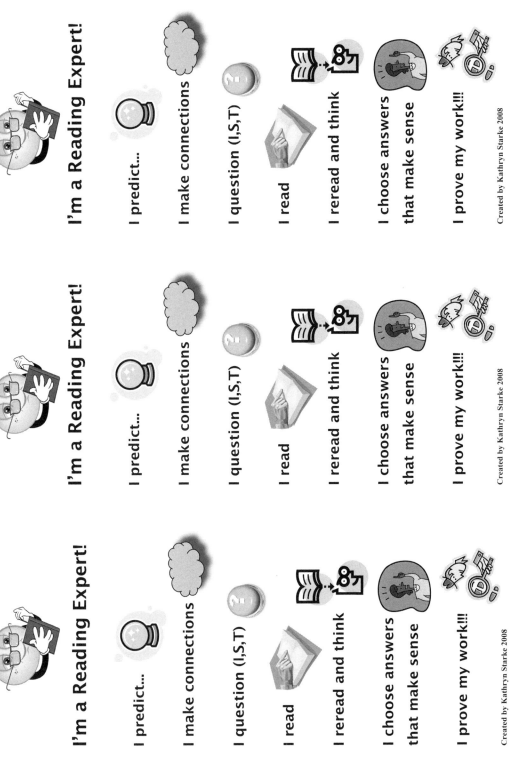

I'm a Reading Expert!

I predict...

I make connections

I question (I,S,T)

I read

I reread and think

I choose answers that make sense

I prove my work!!!

Created by Kathryn Starke 2008

I'm a Reading Expert!

I predict...

I make connections

I question (I,S,T)

I read

I reread and think

I choose answers that make sense

I prove my work!!!

Created by Kathryn Starke 2008

I'm a Reading Expert!

I predict...

I make connections

I question (I,S,T)

I read

I reread and think

I choose answers that make sense

I prove my work!!!

Created by Kathryn Starke 2008

157

excerpt from
BOBBLEHEAD BEATDOWN
(Bo Rush Sports Books)

-- First Practice --

The other Lightning players were already loosening up, tossing footballs and joking around, when Zach raced across the field on his bike. He skidded to a stop, quickly pulling his helmet off the handlebars.

"Nice of you to make it, Fargo!" Chris Rivera laughed and threw a football at Zach.

Zach, still holding the helmet, had to use it as a shield to knock the ball away. "How early did you get here, Chris? Real early, I hope, since you need the extra practice!"

Which wasn't true, since Chris was the best football player he knew. Zach picked up the pigskin and tossed it back to his best friend, but it sailed over Chris's outstretched hand.

"Good thing you're not our QB, Zach."

"Yeah. You do the throwing and I'll do the catching."

Chris retrieved the ball and cocked his arm to fire it to Zach. A whistle pierced the air. All the boys stopped their warm-ups and turned to see Coach MacDuffy standing with his hands on his hips at mid-field.

Chris tucked the football and grinned at Zach, "Ready to rock and roll, amigo?"

"Ready?" Zach nodded and smiled back. "I've been waiting my whole life for this day!"

-- Quarterback to Wide Receiver --

Which wasn't exactly true. Zach didn't even know what

football was until he was four years old. And his dream of playing in the youth majors wasn't really a dream until two years ago -- his first year of organized football in the peewee league.

Two years ago Zach was on the Zephyrs, and the team was so pitiful that the coach actually had Zach playing quarterback. Which wasn't as ridiculous as it sounded because peewee football features a lot more running than passing. And running was Zach's thing. His dad always said he could outrun a cheetah, if they were both wearing cleats.

A couple of the linemen on the Zephyrs, twin brothers and twice Zach's size, were jealous of the rookie quarterback. Max and Dalton Schwartz secretly teased Zach every chance they got, saying the only reason he was quarterback was because his dad was the coach.

That part was true. Zach's dad was the volunteer coach. But that's not why Zach was the starting quarterback. He had proven time and again in wind sprints that he had the fastest wheels on the team. That kind of blazing speed would mean touchdowns once the season started.

But that didn't seem to matter to the annoying Schwartz twins. They kept up a side conversation in the huddle at practice while Zach was trying to call plays.

"Alright, guys. Six veer bootleg shuffle."

Max Schwartz laughed, "What's Peyton Manning whining about now?"

"Probably that he needs his diaper changed," sneered Dalton.

Zach didn't tell his dad about the daily taunts in the huddle. He figured if he was going to run the offense, he needed to act like it didn't bother him.

The Schwartz twins' complaint -- that Zach was the starting quarterback because his dad was the coach -- was proven wrong two days before the season opener. That's when a new kid showed up at practice.

This new kid had just moved to Westridge from Texas. He was nine, just like Zach, but was a head taller. And when Coach

Fargo had the team run wind sprints, Zach found himself in the unusual position of eating a teammate's dust.

That was how he met Chris Rivera. And that was the day Zach became a wide receiver instead of a quarterback.

What Reading Is to Me

by Emily Faris

In ancient Africa, words were thought to have a life-giving force. They believed language was powerful and creative, that words were sacred. There is no separate African linguistic term to distinguish goodness from beauty, because one without the other would negate the whole aesthetic concept. As Yoyo once said, "Reading is dreaming with your eyes open."

Reading has always been an important part of my life. My parents have read to me since I was born, and encouraged me to read all the time. By age three I was a reader and by Kindergarten I was reading chapter books. The innumerable books I've read since then have impacted me in so many ways. I would act out books with my stuffed animals, going on adventures together. For me, reading was the fuel for my imagination. It turned our old rug into a magic carpet, a peach into a flying machine. At night, as I was trying to fall asleep, my mind would wander and come up with stories in my head. To this day, I keep a notepad on my nightstand to write down thoughts, ideas, and questions. I think that books can really have a big impact on your personality. Characters in books inspire me, and are role models for me. I want to be strong like Katniss Everdeen, compassionate like Lina Mayfleet, funny like Connor Lassiter, and smart like Reynie Muldoon. After reading a whole book or series, I feel a personal connection to the characters, and I try to bring out their most positive traits into my life.

Reading has also made me a better writer. In fifth grade, we had the incredible experience of using a student publishing website to create our own books. My story was about a girl coming to America during the 1900s, a topic we had been learning about in school. I had been imagining myself living through it as we learned. And so I wrote about the places my imagination had wandered. After writing and illustrating for weeks, we finally submitted, ordered, and received a hardcover copy of my book. The pride and excitement I had in my work was unlike anything else.

Literature is something that surrounds us everyday, and it's important to learn to appreciate the value of words. There are so many things to learn and places to go when you read a book. What do you want the story of your life to look like?

———————

Emily M. Faris, *tenth grade*

A Reading Limerick

by Mitchel Kirtley

Reading is like watching a television show
Except you have to look at the extra big glow
You have to use imagination
To come up with your own vacation
So grab a very interesting book and grow

Mitchel Kirtley
Ninth grade
Meadowbrook High School
Chesterfield County Public Schools

CLUE GYM

Detective

Name(s)_____

Directions: Read the clues below. You are to figure out what the bold-faced word means using clue words in the sentence. Circle or highlight the clue words that help you. Once you know what the word means, then you can figure out the location described in the actual clue.

On your **CLUE GYM** game board, write the bold-faced word on the line in the correct location box. To complete your game board, you must illustrate a little picture to show what the word means. **Good luck!!!!**

Clue:

1. We read the article in the daily **gazette** that said to bring our rackets here for match.
2. The player decided to **intercept** and make a touchdown here.
3. He had to **guard** the other team member so he could not make a three pointer here.
4. We noticed that tiny white balls were **scattered** all over this green location.
5. The coach began to **scold** a player for using his hands on the ball and another player at this location.
6. The dark alleys in this place started to **illuminate** around the pins.
7. The **monsoon** of wind and rain damaged the bases which caused this location to cancel the game.
8. The **superior** player always scored points when she served the ball in this location.

Tackle Reading by Kathryn Starke, 2016, Creative Minds Publications.
May be copied for classroom use.

——————— **Football Field**	——————— **Bowling Alley**
——————— **Tennis Court**	——————— **Basketball Court**
——————— **Golf Course**	——————— **Soccer Field**
——————— **Volleyball Court**	——————— **Baseball Field**

Name _____

Book _____

Who?	**Where?**

What Happened?

Name _____

Making a Mind Movie

A mind movie is how you visualize the text you are reading.

What is the title of the text, chapter, or chapter book
you are reading?

_____

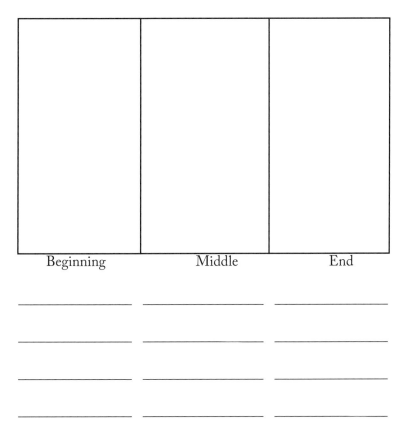

Beginning	Middle	End

_____ _____ _____

_____ _____ _____

_____ _____ _____

_____ _____ _____

My Reading Survey

Name_____   Date_____

1. What is your favorite picture book?

2. What is your favorite chapter book?

3. Do you prefer fiction or nonfiction books?

4. Who would you like to read a biography about?

5. What do you like to learn about from information books?

6. Who is your favorite author?

7. Is reading easy or hard for you?

8. What is one thing you want to learn more about in reading?

9.

Genre Scavenger Hunt

Name _____

Directions: Search through your classroom or home library. Locate one title for each genre listed below.

1. Informational _____

2. Mystery _____

3. Realistic Fiction _____

4. Biography _____

5. Historical Fiction _____

6. Science Fiction _____

7. Fantasy _____

8. Fairy Tale _____

9. Folk Tale/Traditional Literature _____

*Now, choose your favorite book from the library.

Is the book fiction or nonfiction? _____

What is the genre of the book? _____

How do you know? _____

Tackle Reading by Kathryn Starke, 2016, Creative Minds Publications.
May be copied for classroom use.

Contractions, Possessives, and Plurals...Oh My!!

Name _____

Directions: Choose 3 crayon colors. Choose one color to circle all of the contractions. Choose the next color to circle all of the possessives. Choose the final color to circle all of the plurals. Don't let the apostrophe fool you!

hasn't	calendars	wasn't
classmates	they're	Mr. Smith's
students	who's	celebrations
geese	Americans	teacher's
cousins	childrens	berries
girls'	couldn't	Charlie's
Maggie's	she's	won't
isn't	teaches	students'

Tackle Reading by Kathryn Starke, 2016, Creative Minds Publications.
May be copied for classroom use.

Date _____

Dear _____,

    I just finished reading the book _____.

It was about _____

_____.

My favorite part was when _____

_____.

I think you would like it because _____

_____.

Sincerely,

_____

Tackle Reading by Kathryn Starke, 2016, Creative Minds Publications.
May be copied for classroom use.

Tackle Reading Tour

Quality reading instruction goes beyond just reading a book. Urban literacy specialist, Kathryn Starke, will kick off her Tackle Reading Tour for the 2016-2017 school year. She provides literacy coaching and professional development for elementary schools and speaking engagements for parents, families, and community events. Kathryn Starke –successfully turned failing schools into fully accredited in reading in one school year–increased standardized reading scores by 14% in one year, led a school to be number one for language arts teaching in their network, and helped a school get 98% of fourth and fifth graders on or above reading level.

Visit www.creativemindspublications.com to learn more about her literacy services and impact. Book Kathryn Starke today by emailing info@creativemindspublications.com

Creative Minds Publications is a global educational company that exemplifies quality reading instruction for all children. Their mission is to motivate children, support parents, and inspire fellow educators to love teaching reading. Current publications include Amy's Travels, a multicultural children's book that teaches the diversity, geography, and culture of our world. Amy's Travels is in its second edition, third printing, and used in homes and schools in over 26 countries on 6 continents. Turtle Without a Home is an excellent example of environmental literacy recognized as a nature appreciation title and used in environmental educational conferences and school curriculum nationwide.

THANK YOU PAGE

Tackle Reading has been created and donated to Title I
elementary schools nationwide thanks to the generosity
of the following people.

Arlise Carson, ASMC, LLC
BeyondtheLaces.com
Brandylane Publishers
Charles Johnson Foundation
Geico
Henrico Education Foundation
Teespring
The Singletary Network NY